FAMOUS AIRCRAFT
OF ALL TIME

FAMOUS AIRCRAFT OF ALL TIME

KENNETH MUNSON

ILLUSTRATED BY
JOHN W. WOOD
BRIAN HILEY
WILLIAM HOBSON
JACK PELLING
EUSLIN BRUCE

ARCO PUBLISHING COMPANY, INC.
New York

Published 1977 by Arco Publishing Company, Inc.
219 Park Avenue South, New York, N.Y. 10003

Copyright © Blandford Press Ltd 1976

Printed in Great Britain

Library of Congress Cataloging in Publication Data

Munson, Kenneth G.
  Famous aircraft of all time.

  (Arco color series)
  Includes index.
  1. Airplanes—History. I. Title.
TL670.3.M86   1977   629.133'34'09   76-30686
ISBN 0-668-04224-9
ISBN 0-668-04230-3 pbk.

CONTENTS

PREFACE AND ACKNOWLEDGEMENTS

Great? Historic? Significant? Famous? When this book was first suggested, each one of these adjectives was considered for the aircraft to be included. Each produced a different list of aircraft selected, and it was soon apparent that, whichever list of aircraft was adopted, it would be certain to please some readers and disappoint others. For better or worse, the eventual selection is now offered, in the hope that it will at least please 'some of the people all of the time'; and, for those readers who do not find their own particular choice included, I can only offer my apologies in advance – with the consolation (if it is one) that not all of my own favourites found a place on the final list either!

In the preparation of the colour plates, once again ably executed by Jack Wood and his team of artists, acknowledgement is gratefully recorded of material published at various times in *Aeroplane Monthly*; Aircraft Profiles (various); the *Journal* of the American Aviation Historical Society; the *Journal* of Cross & Cockade (Great Britain); *Flight International*; *History of Aviation*; the I.P.M.S. magazines of Australasia, Canada, the U.K. and U.S.A.; and *The Koku-Fan*. The Guinness Superlatives publication *Air Facts and Feats* was of tremendous assistance in checking much of the data concerning individual aircraft, as also was *Jane's 100 Significant Aircraft 1909–1969*. Of the individuals who helped in so many different ways, I should like particularly to thank Giorgio Apostolo of the Italian Aviation Research Branch of Air-Britain; Chaz Bowyer; Barrington J. Gray; Ian Huntley; David Kemp of British Caledonian Airways; Donald S. Lopez, Assistant Director of Aeronautics at the National Air and Space Museum in Washington; John W. R. Taylor; and, not least, Mrs Lynne Crowfoot of Blandford Press, for stepping into the breach at the last moment to type the manuscript.

K.M.

Seaford, Sussex
Spring 1976

HISTORICAL BACKGROUND

'In 1901, I confess that I said to my brother Orville that man would not fly for fifty years. Two years later we made flights. This demonstration of my impotence as a prophet gave me such a shock that ever more I have distrusted myself and avoided all predictions.' So said Wilbur Wright in 1908; yet one prediction which he could have made with absolute certainty was that the Flyer I, on which he and his brother made four tentative flights on 17 December 1903, at Kitty Hawk, North Carolina, would from then onward rank as the most famous aircraft of all time. 'Since then,' as Sir Peter Masefield wrote on the 70th anniversary of that flight, 'in the space of one "Standard, Mark One, Human Lifetime", the art and the science of flying, and the whole business of aeronautics, has evolved from a brief series of "one-man-straights" to become a self-confident commercial giant which circles the Earth, an industry in the forefront of technology, a major employer and user of capital – a focus of social change.' The aircraft portrayed and described in this book provide an opportunity to trace that evolution through some of the milestones along the road which aviation has travelled since 1903, and some of the famous aircraft that have made that evolution possible.

To begin with, to the Wright brothers themselves must be given the credit for leading aviation beyond their own initial achievement of four 'one-man-straights'. 'It seemed to my brother and myself,' said Wilbur Wright in 1901, 'that the main reason why the problem (of gliding) had remained so long unsolved was that no one had been able to obtain any adequate practice.' As recorded elsewhere in this book, the Wrights' own practice amounted to more than 2,000 flights in three years in their gliders, before they directed their attention to the two other main problems that had thwarted everyone before them: the application of power, and the mastery of control in the air. The first of these was overcome in the Flyer I, but it was not until their Flyer III of 1905 that they were satisfied with their achievement of the second, the most important requirement of all, and for that reason the 1905 machine was chosen as the starting-point for this book. Able to turn, bank and perform figure-of-eight manoeuvres in the air, it was the next step forward from flying 'straights'. By 1908 it was possible to refer to the current Wright biplane as the 'standard type'; and on 14 May of that year one of these machines went beyond the 'one-man' stage by carrying its first passenger. From such modest beginnings have come the 500-passenger-carrying 'Jumbo' jets of the seventies.

The aeroplane had now been proved able to fly, and safe enough to fly with a passenger. But flights of endurance round and round the borders of a safe airfield were all very well, but were of limited practical value: it next had to prove its ability to convey people from one place to another. In promoting this next step forward, a considerable debt must be acknowledged to the far-sighted Lord Northcliffe who, through the medium of his newspaper, the *Daily Mail*, put up handsome money prizes to provide the incentive for such flights; and it is no coincidence that the names most associated with these events, those of Louis Blériot and Henry Farman, should be the two greatest in the early history of European aviation. Blériot's cross-Channel flight from France to England, in particular, made a staggering public impact and gave, for the first time, a real hint of what the aeroplane might mean as a future weapon of war. Both men, as a result of the achievements of their aeroplanes, were able to establish companies to manufacture them on a commercial scale which, if not yet in the realms of mass production, at least earned them an extremely comfortable living. Aviation had begun to become an industry, within only six years of that historic flight at Kitty Hawk.

It was only another five years before that embryo industry received another boost, this time from the entirely unwelcome impetus of a major European war. Early beliefs that aeroplanes had only a limited usefulness, for communications or to 'spot' for the artillery, were very quickly dispelled, and their place taken by an entirely new facet of warfare – aerial combat. Thus were born the first bombers and gun-carrying fighters, among which several classic designs began to emerge, especially after the evolution of synchronising gear by means of which a machine-gun could be made to fire through the blades of a turning propeller without hitting them. The first such fighter, the

Fokker Eindecker, had a field day while it was the only type on the Western Front with such an armament; but, once its opponents began to be similarly armed, other factors such as speed, climb and manoeuvrability became of more importance. Technology was on the move. So, too, was the industrial side of aviation: realisation of the value of air power brought production contracts measured in thousands of aircraft, instead of tens or hundreds.

With the ending of World War 1, aviation found itself at a crossroads: a large and thriving industry with, suddenly, its principal customers no longer in business. Many aircraft-manufacturing companies did not survive, others were obliged to diversify into non-aviation fields in order to do so, and it was to be several years before the impetus was regained. In the meantime, attention focused again upon spectacular flights such as the attempts to cross the Atlantic by air and the outstanding round-the-world flight in 1924 by the Douglas World Cruisers. Prestige or prize money may have provided the spur which made such flights possible, but there was an underlying practical value which began to emerge in the twenties, for they laid the foundations of the airline route networks that were to follow later.

Technologically, perhaps, the early twenties were a sterile period in aircraft development, for obvious reasons. They were, however, notable for two things. One, already mentioned, was the beginning of the commercial airlines, albeit a shaky beginning based largely upon the use of converted wartime bombers. The other was the beginning of an attempt to bring the pleasures of flying to the public at large on a more personal basis than that of simply buying an airline ticket. This was the era of the aerial circus, the 'barnstormers' and the 'five-bob-flip' – and, in due time, of the flying club movement. Hundreds of war-surplus trainers such as the Avro 504 and the Curtiss 'Jenny' were bought by ex-pilots and others and used nationwide to give spectacular flying displays and joy-rides and make the public 'air-minded', and many a pilot of later years can trace his first acquaintance with flying to just such an event. From the mid-1920s the establishment of flying clubs blossomed, particularly after the appearance of such delightful private-owner aeroplanes as the little de Havilland Moth and, a few years later, the Taylor Cub.

By the end of the twenties, technology had begun to move forward again, if slowly at first. Airliners like the Fokker and Ford tri-motors were now custom-designed for their job, and Lindbergh's ecstatic reception in Paris far outstripped that afforded by the English to Blériot eighteen years before. But, more than any of these, the 1931 world flight by Wiley Post and Harold Gatty foreshadowed the coming revolution in aeroplane design. Their Lockheed Vega, one of the famous family of 'plywood bullets' produced by this American company, was a beautifully streamlined monoplane with tremendous strength and reliability. Within only a few years it was to be followed by sleek, all-metal monoplanes with cantilever wings, retractable undercarriages, supercharged engines, variable-pitch propellers and other significant improvements, all contributing to a great stride forward in performance.

A leader in this progress was the Boeing company, whose YB-9 bomber prototype and single-engined Monomail led to the Model 247, first of this new generation of fast and comfortable transport aircraft to enter airline service; and it is a measure of the rate at which aircraft design was now progressing that it was itself outmoded by the Douglas DC-1 within a year of doing so. Not that the day of the biplane was yet over, by any means. Imperial Airways never had a safer or more popular airliner than the giant H.P.42 which, despite its 'built-in headwinds', served right through the 1930s; and the Royal Air Force had few better aircraft in the inter-war years than the ubiquitous Hawker Hart. Indeed, it was a descendant of a descendant of the Hart that brought the monoplane age to British military aviation, in the shape of the Hurricane fighter.

The 'focus of social change' of which Sir Peter Masefield wrote had by now become manifest: air travel was a safe, accepted and 'respectable' means of getting from one place to another. Aviation had become self-confident, too, and had circled the Earth – or, at least, individual intrepid fliers had done so: it would be some time yet before this became part of the standard airline pattern of operation. In the meantime, Europe – and the rest of the world – had to undergo the trauma of another major war.

Once again, this gave added impetus to aeronautical progress, to meet the need for greater speeds, better armament, bigger bomb loads and longer ranges; and in the process (though they are beyond the scope of this book) some fairly bizarre solutions were offered. On

4

the conventional level, however, the period 1939–45 saw the piston-engined warplane pushed virtually to the limit of its development, with fighter speeds approaching close to 500 m.p.h. (805 km/hr.) and bombs of up to 22,000 lb. (9,980 kg.) in size being carried by a single specially-modified Lancaster; and it saw the start of the next revolution in aviation – the arrival of the 'jet age'.

The immediate effect of jet and rocket engines was to offer the possibility of greatly increased speeds, and almost immediately aircraft designers and test pilots came up against a new phenomenon: the so-called 'sound barrier', or the effects of compressibility upon an airframe caused by the build-up of shock waves as the aircraft approached the speed of sound. For a while this barrier seemed impassable, and several good aeroplanes and valuable test pilots were lost in the attempt, but again the technological problem was met and overcome. To today's designers, supersonic aeroplanes come as naturally as subsonic ones did to the generations before them, but thirty years ago that 'barrier' appeared to be a very real one indeed. In that context it is worth recalling the more recent words of U.S. Air Force Captain Charles ('Chuck') Yeager who, on 14 October 1947 in the Bell X-1, became the first man successfully to fly faster than the speed of sound: 'I've tried to think back to that first flight past Mach 1, but it doesn't seem any more important than any of the others. I was at about 37,000, straight, level, and it was just a matter of flying the airplane. It flew very nicely and got up to 0·97 on the Mach indicator, and then the meter jumped to about 1·05 as I accelerated past the shock wave that was on the nose of the airplane. I was kind of disappointed that it wasn't more of a big charge than it was.'

The development of jet and rocket engines, although started in several countries before World War 2, owes a large debt to the work in these fields carried out by German technologists during the war years, the results of which – and many of the scientists associated with it – were snapped up by the victorious powers in 1945. Britain, in particular, was able to develop an early lead in gas-turbine engines, enabling it to give the world both the first jet airliner (the Comet) and the first turboprop airliner (the Viscount). Largely due to a succession of political idiocies, it was a lead that soon became eroded or given away; one such act, the sale of Rolls-Royce Nene engines to the Soviet Union, enabled that country to put into the Korean War of

1950–53 such an excellent fighter as the MiG-15, one of the first participants in jet *v*. jet air combat.

With Mach 1 successfully surpassed, it was a matter of time rather than technology before Mach 2 became the order of the day, and three of the best fighters in this performance bracket are featured in this book. At the time of writing only two in-service aircraft in the world are capable of sustained flight at Mach 3 or beyond: the Lockheed SR-71 strategic reconnaissance aircraft, and the fighter/reconnaissance MiG-25 from the Soviet Union; and still in a class of its own, although no longer flying, is the North American X-15, which at Mach 6·72 is the fastest manned vehicle to have flown within the Earth's atmosphere. Equally unique, though in a quite different way, is the vertical take-off Hawker Siddeley P.1127/Kestrel/Harrier, whose Rolls-Royce (originally Bristol Siddeley) Pegasus vectored-thrust turbofan engine brought a whole new concept in aircraft propulsion and military tactics. Completing the selection for this book are the Boeing 747 – typifying Masefield's 'self-confident commercial giant' – and the Anglo-French Concorde which, perhaps more than any aircraft before it, typifies 'an industry in the forefront of technology, a major employer and user of capital, and a focus of social change'.

Sir Peter wrote also of 'the art and science' of flying, and it is perhaps when these two forces are blended best that the greatest aeroplanes result. Very few of the famous aircraft in this book could be described as less than handsome, and many are among the most aesthetically appealing ever built; and for this reason, if for no other, an effort has been made to give credit to the designers of many of them in the individual descriptions. Nor is it any coincidence that the names of some of the world's greatest aero-engines recur among the aircraft data: the Rolls-Royce Merlin and the Pratt & Whitney Wasp family appear no less than five times each, and the Gnome rotaries, the American Liberty and the Wright Whirlwind three times each.

Fame is an elusive commodity to define, and no two dictionaries will define it in the same way. Sometimes it will last for generations, sometimes it is no more than a nine days' wonder. Sometimes it brings great acclaim, sometimes only notoriety. But in one way or another, each of the aircraft in this book has staked its own claim for inclusion among the famous examples of its kind.

One apology – or, at least. explanation – remains to be made: for the absence from this book of any helicopters or other rotorcraft. This was not because no aircraft of this type was thought to be worthy of inclusion – far from it – but purely for reasons of space. Whether that decision was a correct one the reader must be left to judge for himself.

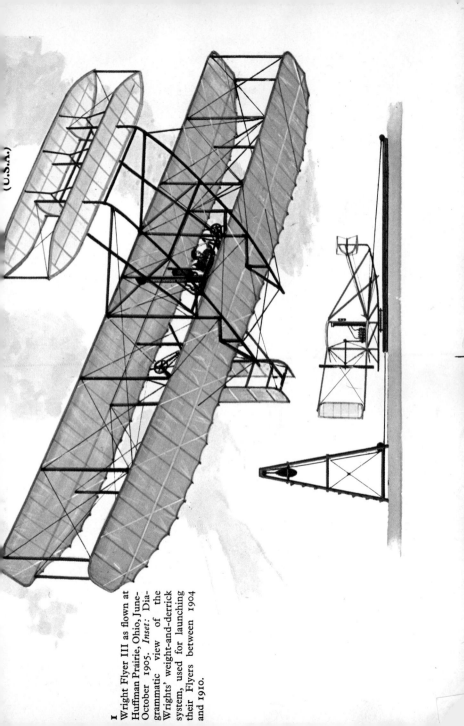

(U.S.A.)

I Wright Flyer III as flown at Huffman Prairie, Ohio, June-October 1905. *Inset:* Diagrammatic view of the Wrights' weight-and-derrick system, used for launching their Flyers between 1904 and 1910.

BLÉRIOT XI (France)

2
Modified Type XI monoplane in which Louis Blériot made the first aeroplane crossing of the English Channel on 25 July 1909. Map shows the route followed by Blériot.

HENRY FARMAN III (France)

Henry Farman III (shown being erected) flown by Claude Grahame-White from London to Manchester on 27-28 April 1910. *Inset:* Another view of Grahame-White's Farman.

CURTISS HYDRO-AEROPLANE (U.S.A.)

4
Curtiss Hydro-aeroplane in initial form with wide central float and pusher propeller. *Inset:* The Hydro-aeroplane in its second form, with long central float and tractor propeller.

5 Prototype Avro 504 during coastal tour of Great Britain, summer 1914. *Inset:* Avro 504N with blind-flying hood over rear cockpit.

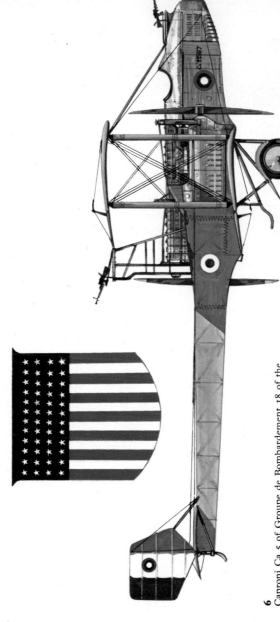

6

Caproni Ca 5 of Groupe de Bombardement 18 of the Italian Air Service (with both Italian and U.S. insignia), *ca.* September 1918. *Inset:* U.S. shield insignia believed carried by the Ca 3 of Fiorello La Guardia, in charge of training U.S. Caproni aircrew at Foggia in 1917-18.

7
de Havilland (Airco) D.H.2 of No. 24 Squadron R.F.C. (possibly that flown by 2nd Lt D. M. Tidmarsh), spring 1916. *Inset:* Nose detail, showing forward-firing Lewis gun; the windshield was fixed on to the gun mounting.

FOKKER EINDECKER (Germany)

8

Fokker E.III which force-landed behind British lines in France on 8 April 1916; now in the possession of the Science Museum, London. *Inset:* Inboard profile of E.III structure. Note the spherical fuel tank aft of the pilot's seat.

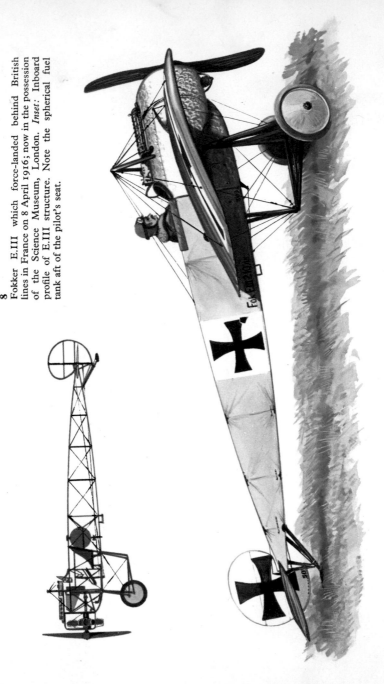

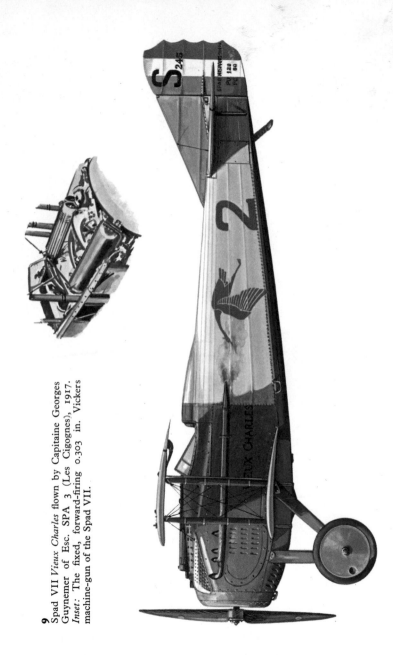

9
Spad VII *Vieux Charles* flown by Capitaine Georges
Guynemer of Esc. SPA 3 (Les Cigognes), 1917.
Inset: The fixed, forward-firing 0.303 in. Vickers
machine-gun of the Spad VII.

ALBATROS D.III
(Germany)

10
Oeffag-built Albatros D.III (Series 153) flown by Hauptmann Godwin Brumowski of the Ö.U. Fliegertruppe, Istrien Sesana, March 1918.

Right: **NIEUPORT 17**
(France)

11
Nieuport Nie. 17C.1 flown by Lt Charles Nungesser of Esc. N 3, summer/autumn 1917.

12
Whitehead-built de Havilland D.H.9A of No. 30 Squadron R.A.F., Iraq, *ca.* 1926-27. *Inset:* Insignia of No. 30 Squadron, as painted on the aircraft's rear fuselage.

BRISTOL FIGHTER (U.K.)

13
Bristol F.2B Fighter of No. 139 Squadron R.A.F., Villaverla, Italy, September 1918. *Inset:* Observer's 0.303 in. Lewis machine-gun on Scarff ring mounting.

14
Fokker Dr.I in which Rittmeister Manfred von
Richthofen of JG.I was killed on 21 April 1918.
Inset: The cowling decoration of the Fokker Dr.I
in which Leutnant Werner Voss of Jasta 10 was shot
down on 23 September 1917.

Right: **SOPWITH CAMEL (U.K.)**

15
Sopwith Camel F.I flown by Major Raymond Collishaw, C.O. of No. 18 Squadron R.N.A.S., autumn 1917.

Below: **FOKKER D.VII (Germany)**

16
Fokker D.VII flown by Oblt Ernst Udet of Jasta 4, 1918.

NAVY CURTISS NC-TA (U.S.A.)

17
Navy-Curtiss NC-TA (NC-4) which made the first aeroplane crossing of the North Atlantic, 16-31 May 1919. Map shows the route of NC-4's trans-Atlantic journey.

VICKERS VIMY (U.K.)

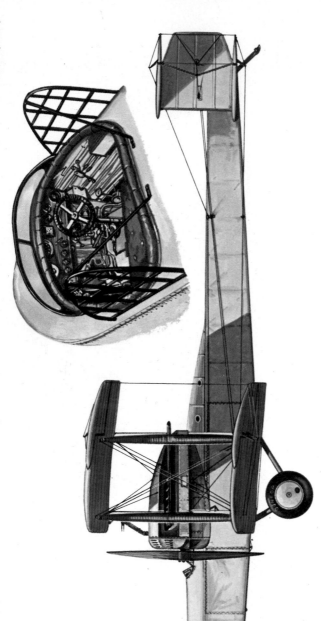

18
Vickers Vimy flown by Capt John Alcock and Lt
Arthur Whitten Brown on the first non-stop flight
across the Atlantic, 14-15 June 1919. *Inset:* The
trans-Atlantic Vimy's simply-instrumented double
cockpit. Alcock (pilot) sat on the right, Brown
(navigator) on the left.

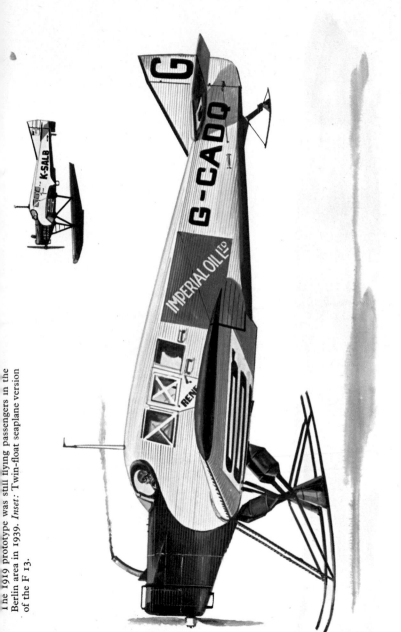

The 1919 prototype was still flying passengers in the Berlin area in 1939. *Inset:* Twin-float seaplane version of the F 13.

DORNIER WAL (Germany)

20

Dornier Do J Wal *Valencia* of the Spanish Navy, 1926. Cabral and Coutinho's *Plus Ultra* was similar except for its engines. *Inset:* Dornier 10-ton Wal D-AKER *Taifun* of Deutsche Luft Hansa on ship's catapult, *ca.* 1936.

21
Douglas World Cruiser No. 4 *New Orleans*, April-September 1924. Map shows the route taken in the DWC's round-the-world flight in 1924. A full itinerary is given in Appendix I.

DE HAVILLAND GIPSY MOTH (U.K.)

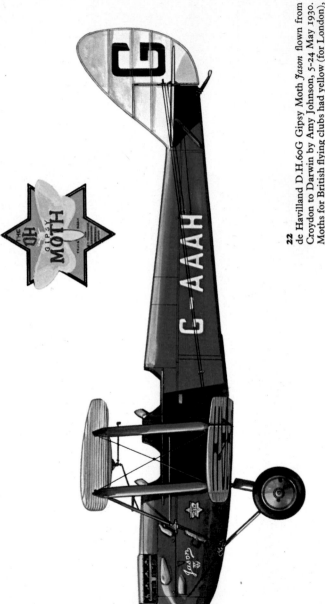

22 de Havilland D.H.60G Gipsy Moth *Jason* flown from Croydon to Darwin by Amy Johnson, 5-24 May 1930. Moths for British flying clubs had yellow (for London), red (for Newcastle), green (for Midlands) or blue and silver paint schemes (Lancashire). *Inset:* The de Havilland 'Moth' emblem.

Below: **FOKKER D.VII (Germany)**

23
Fokker F.VIIb-3m *Southern Cross*, in which Charles Kingsford Smith and crew made the first air crossing of the Tasman Sea on 10-11 September 1928. *Inset:* Fokker company logo.

FORD TRI-MOTOR
(U.S.A.)

24
Ford Model 4-AT-B tri-motor *Floyd Bennett* which, on 28-29 November 1929, became the first aeroplane to fly over the South Pole, carrying the famous Polar explorer Lt Cdr Richard Byrd. Map shows the route of the South Polar flight.

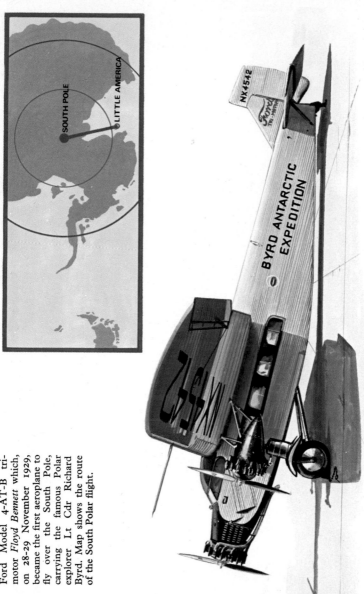

25
Ryan NYP *Spirit of St. Louis* flown from New York to Paris by Charles A. Lindbergh, 20-21 May 1927. Lindbergh's instrument panel is shown as a line drawing near the end of this book. *Inset*: The Ryan company's 'flying R' emblem on the *Spirit's* fin.

LOCKHEED VEGA
(U.S.A.)

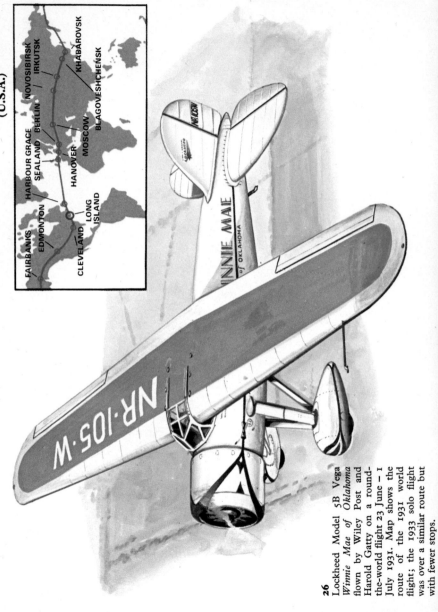

FAIRBANKS
EDMONTON
HARBOUR GRACE
SEALAND BERLIN
NOVOSIBIRSK IRKUTSK
KHABAROVSK
BLAGOVESHCHENSK
MOSCOW
HANOVER
CLEVELAND
LONG ISLAND

NR·105·W

WINNIE MAE
OF OKLAHOMA

26
Lockheed Model 5B Vega *Winnie Mae of Oklahoma* flown by Wiley Post and Harold Gatty on a round-the-world flight 23 June – 1 July 1931. Map shows the route of the 1931 world flight; the 1933 solo flight was over a similar route but with fewer stops.

27
Hawker Hart I Bomber of No. 57 (Bomber) Squadron
R.A.F., Upper Heyford, 1934. *Inset:* The observer's
0.303 in. ring-mounted Lewis machine-gun on the
Hart, a movable weapon with seven 97-round drums
of ammunition provided (not shown in the main
illustration).

28

Handley Page H.P.42W *Helena* of Imperial Airways Ltd., *ca.* 1932. This view makes it easy to see how the H.P.42 got the nickname 'flying banana'. *Inset:* Nose of G-AAXE *Hengist*, with civil air ensign and GPO Royal Mail pennant.

29
Junkers Ju 52/3m g3e of I/KG 152 'Hindenburg',
Greifswald, mid-1936. Its career as a bomber was
short-lived, but it became one of the most famous
transport aircraft ever built. *Inset*: The retractable
ventral gun/bomb-aiming 'dustbin' of the Junkers Ju
52/3m bombers.

TAYLOR/PIPER CUB
(U.S.A.)

30 Piper L-21B (PA-18-135) Super Cub of No. 299 Squadron, Groep Lichte Vliegtuigen, Royal Netherlands Air Force, Soesterberg, *ca.* 1973. *Left:* Early production Taylor Cub, 1932.

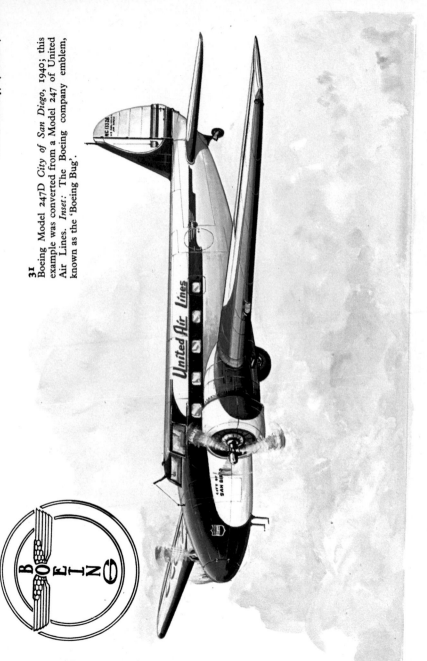

BOEING 247 (U.S.A.)

31
Boeing Model 247D *City of San Diego*, 1940; this example was converted from a Model 247 of United Air Lines. *Inset:* The Boeing company emblem, known as the 'Boeing Bug'.

TUPOLEV ANT-25 (U.S.S.R.)

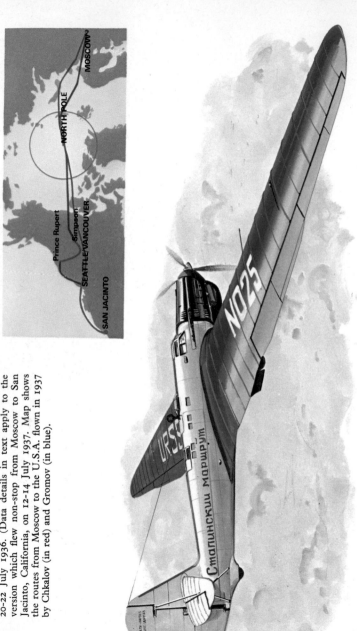

32
TsAGI RD (Tupolev ANT-25) which made an attempt on the world closed-circuit distance record, 20-22 July 1936. (Data details in text apply to the version which flew non-stop from Moscow to San Jacinto, California, on 12-14 July 1937. Map shows the routes from Moscow to the U.S.A. flown in 1937 by Chkalov (in red) and Gromov (in blue).

DOUGLAS DC-3 (U.S.A.)

33
Douglas R4D-5 *Que Sera Sera* of U.S. Navy Squadron VX-6 (Air Development Squadron Six), which on 31 October 1956 became the first aeroplane to land at the South Pole. *Inset:* Badge of 'Operation Deep Freeze'.

Below: **DORNIER Do 17** (Germany)

Left: **POLIKARPOV I-15** (U.S.S.R.)

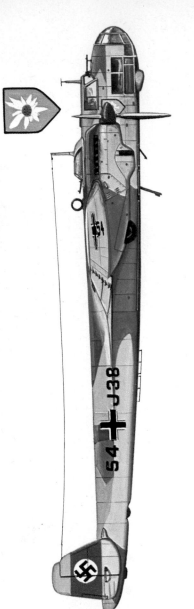

34
Dornier Do 17 E-1 of 8./KG 255, Memmingen, *ca.* 1938.

Inset (right): The Geschwader emblem of KG 255.

35
Polikarpov I-153 *Chaika* of the Soviet Air Force in Finland, spring 1942.

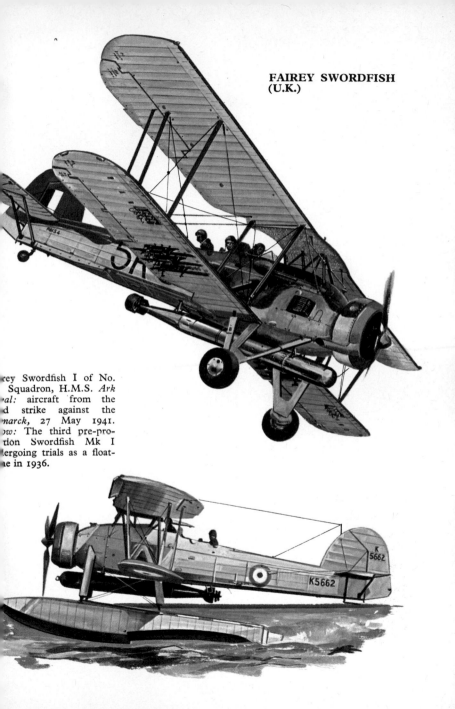

**FAIREY SWORDFISH
(U.K.)**

...rey Swordfish I of No.
... Squadron, H.M.S. *Ark
...al:* aircraft from the
...d strike against the
...narck, 27 May 1941.
...w: The third pre-pro-
...tion Swordfish Mk I
...ergoing trials as a float-
...e in 1936.

DE HAVILLAND COMET (U.K.)

37 de Havilland D.H.88 Comet *Grosvenor House* flown by C.W.A. Scott and T. Campbell Black to win the 'MacRobertson' England-New Zealand air race, 20-23 October 1934. Map shows the route of the 1934 'MacRobertson' air race.

Breslau, late 1937/early 1938. *Inset:* Rear-mounted MG 15 machine-gun of the Ju 87 A.

39 North American AT-6 (Sk 16) of F10 Wing, Royal Swedish Air Force, Angelholm, May 1970. *Inset:* Schulz's cartoon character 'Snoopy', as painted on

40

Boeing B-17G Flying Fortress of the 447th Bomb Group, U.S. Eighth Air Force, Rattlesden, Suffolk, 1944. *Inset*: Bendix powered 'chin' turret of the B-17G, with two 0.50 in. M-2 Browning machine-guns.

MARTIN M-130 (U.S.A.)

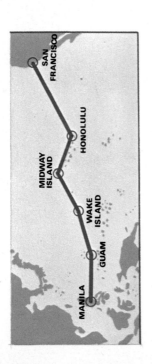

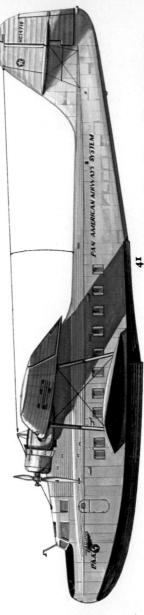

41
Martin M-130 *China Clipper* of Pan American Airways System, autumn 1935. Map shows the route of the inaugural flight for the trans-Pacific air mail service, 22 November to 6 December 1935.

MESSERSCHMITT Bf 109 (Germany)

42
Messerschmitt Bf 109 F-2 of 7./JG 54 'Grünherz',
Leningrad area, winter 1941-42. Best of all versions
of this aircraft, the Bf 109 F first flew on 10 July
1940. *Inset:* Gruppe emblem of III./JG 54.

HAWKER HURRICANE (U.K.)

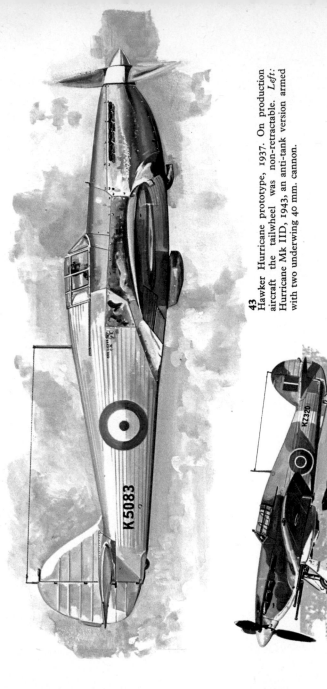

43
Hawker Hurricane prototype, 1937. On production aircraft the tailwheel was non-retractable. *Left:* Hurricane Mk IID, 1943, an anti-tank version armed with two underwing 40 mm. cannon.

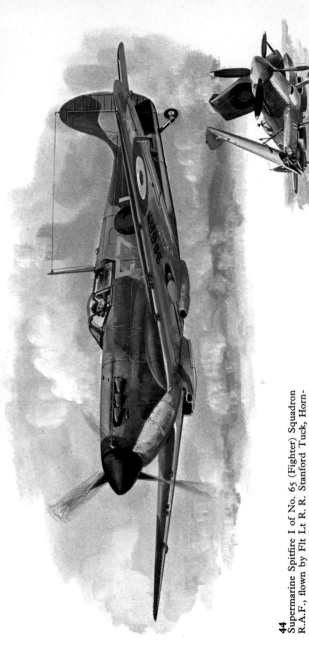

44
Supermarine Spitfire I of No. 65 (Fighter) Squadron R.A.F., flown by Flt Lt R. R. Stanford Tuck, Hornchurch, mid-1939. From 1936, the Spitfire and Seafire stayed in continuous production until 1947. *Inset*: Prototype Seafire III, late 1942.

MITSUBISHI KARIGANE (Japan)

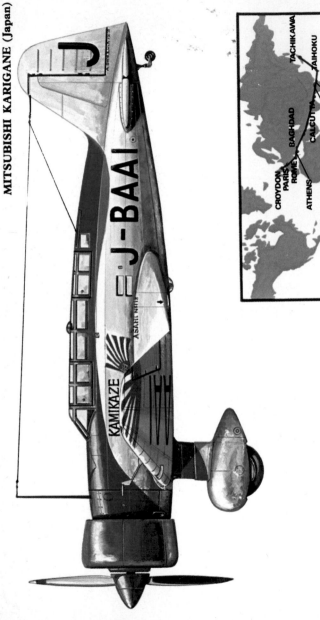

45
Mitsubishi Karigane I *Kamikaze*, which flew from Tachikawa to Croydon 6-9 April 1937. Map shows the itinerary of the Tachikawa-Croydon flight.

Short S.23 'C' class *Coogee* of Qantas Empire Airways, 1938. Map shows routes operated in 1938 by 'C' class flying-boats of Imperial Airways (blue) and Qantas Empire Airways (red).

MITSUBISHI 'ZERO' (Japan)

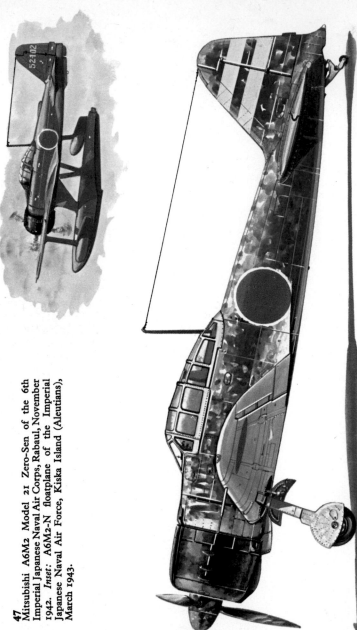

47
Mitsubishi A6M2 Model 21 Zero-Sen of the 6th
Imperial Japanese Naval Air Corps, Rabaul, November
1942. *Inset:* A6M2-N floatplane of the Imperial
Japanese Naval Air Force, Kiska Island (Aleutians),
March 1943.

FOCKE-WULF Fw 190 (Germany)

48
Focke-Wulf Fw 190 D-9 in typical Luftwaffe home
defence colour scheme, spring 1945. Only a handful
of Fw 190s now survive from some 20,000 built.
Inset: Cockpit interior of an Fw 190 A.

ILYUSHIN Il-2 (U.S.S.R.)

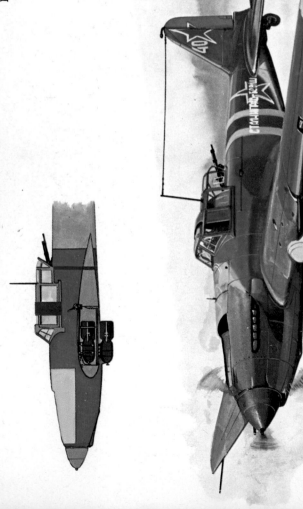

49

Ilyushin Il-2m3 of the Soviet Air Force, Berlin, May 1945. *Inset:* Internal/external bomb stowage and armour protection: 6 mm. armour shell (turquoise); 13 mm. armour plate (dark blue); 8 mm. steel plate (purple); and 55/65 mm. armoured glass windscreen (grey). Pale blue portion is 5 mm. duralumin; rear of fuselage is wooden or duralumin monocoque.

NORTH AMERICAN MUSTANG (U.S.A.)

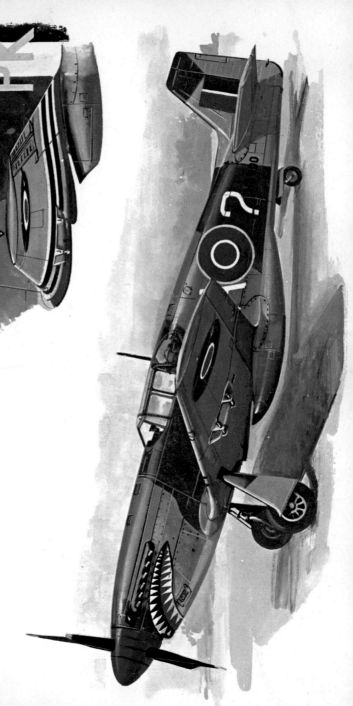

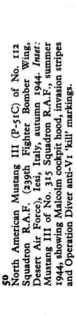

50
North American Mustang III (P-51C) of No. 112
Squadron R.A.F. (239th Fighter Bomber Wing,
Desert Air Force), Iesi, Italy, autumn 1944. *Inset:*
Mustang III of No. 315 Squadron R.A.F., summer
1944, showing Malcolm cockpit hood, invasion stripes
and Operation Diver anti-V1 'kill' markings.

DE HAVILLAND
MOSQUITO (U.K.)

51 de Havilland Mosquito F.B.XVIII of No. 248 Squadron Special Detachment R.A.F., Portreath, June 1944. *Inset:* Mosquito P.R. XVI.

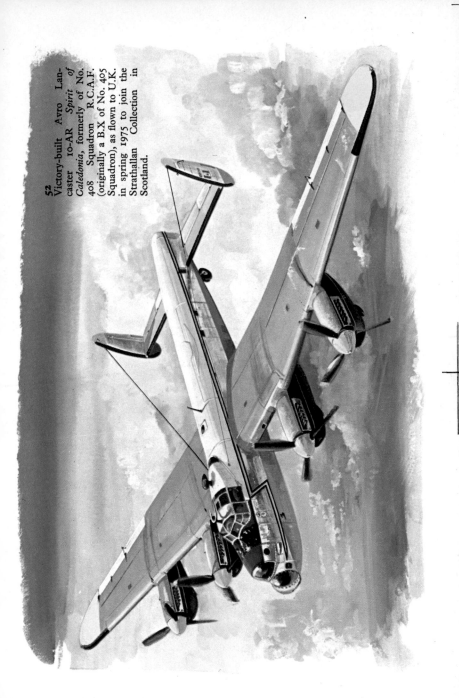

52
Victory-built Avro Lancaster 10-AR *Spirit of Caledonia*, formerly of No. 408 Squadron R.C.A.F. (originally a B.X of No. 405 Squadron), as flown to U.K. in spring 1975 to join the Strathallan Collection in Scotland.

MESSERSCHMITT
Me 262 (Germany)

53
Messerschmitt Me 262 B-1a/
U1 two-seat radar-equipped
night fighter of Kommando
Welter (later 10./NJG 11),
Berlin, spring 1945. *Left:*
Single-seat Me 262 A-1a
flown by Oberstleutnant
Heinz Bär of II./EJG 2,
Lechfeld, March 1945.

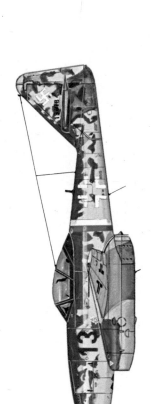

54
Lockheed Model 649 Constellation of Eastern Air Lines, fitted with ventral 'Speedpak', 1947. The 'Speedpak' reduced the Constellation's speed by only 12 m.p.h. (20 km/hr). *Inset*: Emblem of Eastern Air Lines.

55
First Bell X-1A, *ca.* 1954. *Inset:* Launch of the
first X-1 from a B-50 carrier aircraft, 1947.

AMERICAN SABRE
(U.S.A.)

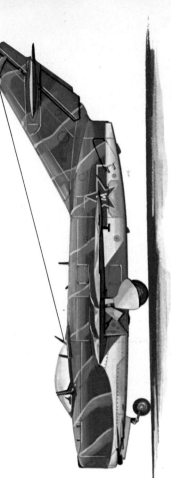

57
North American F-86F Sabre of the U.S. Air Force 335th Fighter Interception Squadron, Korea, *ca.* 1952-53.

Right: **MIKOYAN/ GUREVICH MiG-15 (U.S.S.R.).**

56
Mikoyan/Gurevich MiG-15*bis* of the Air Force of the Chinese People's Liberation Army, Korea, *ca.* 1953.

BOEING STRATOJET
(U.S.A.)

58
Boeing B-47E Stratojet of Strategic Air Command,
U.S. Air Force, *ca.* 1955. *Inset*: Close-up of nose band
and insignia of Strategic Air Command.

VICKERS VISCOUNT (U.K.)

59
Vickers Viscount Type 761 (Series 700D), ex Union of Burma Airways, prior to lease by Middle East Airlines in 1963. *Inset:* Insignia of Middle East Airlines.

HAWKER SIDDELEY COMET (U.K.)

Hawker Siddeley Comet 4C of Sudan Airways, 1963.
Inset: The de Havilland D.H.108 experimental
swept-wing aircraft, originally intended as a half-
scale testbed for a tail-less D.H.106 design.

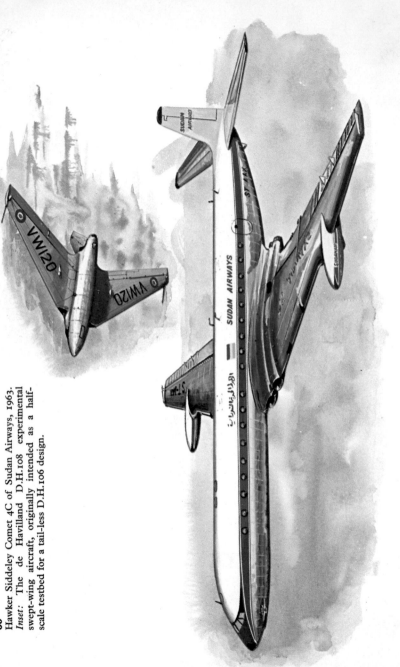

61
Canadair-built Lockheed
CF-104 Starfighter of No.
439 (Sabre Toothed Tiger)
Squadron, Canadian Armed
Forces, during 'Tiger Meet'
at Woodbridge, England, 4-7
August 1969. *Inset.* Detail of
tiger's head on forward fuselage.

BOEING 707 (U.S.A.)

PAN AM

62
Boeing Model 367-80 (707
prototype), summer 1954.
Inset: Insignia of Pan American Airways, first airline to

MIRAGE (France)

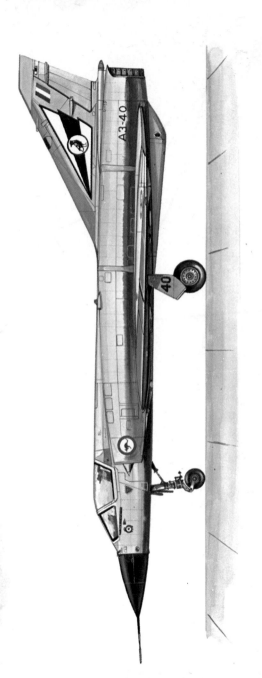

63
CAC-built CA-29 (Dassault Mirage III-O (F)) of No. 75 Squadron R.A.A.F., Butterworth, Malaysia, spring 1968. *Left:* The Israel Aircraft Industries Kfir, developed from the Mirage.

McDONNELL DOUGLAS PHANTOM II
(U.S.A.)

64
McDonnell Douglas F-4EJ Phantom II of the 301st Tactical Fighter Squadron, Japan Air Self-Defence Force, Hyakuri, 1974. *Inset:* Another view of the same aircraft.

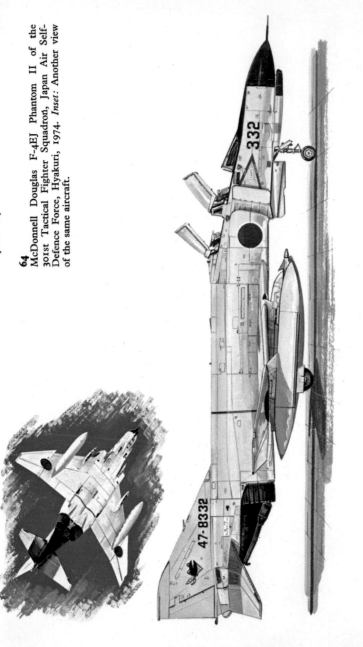

**NORTH AMERICAN
X-15 (U.S.A.)**

65
North American X-15A-2
research aircraft, *ca.* 1964.
Inset: The X-15 in its
launching position beneath
the wing of its B-52 carrier
aircraft.

HAWKER SIDDELEY P.1127/KESTREL (U.K.)

66
Hawker Siddeley Kestrel
F(GA) Mk.1, first of nine
aircraft built for tripartite
evaluation squadron, 1964.
Inset: Insignia of the British/

BOEING 747 (U.S.A.)

67
Boeing Model 747-217B in the insignia of CP Air, 1974-75. *Inset:* Insignia of CP Air.

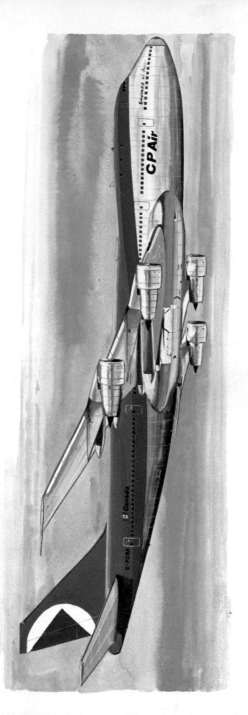

CONCORDE
(France/U.K.)

68
Aérospatiale/BAC Concorde in British Airways livery. *Inset:* Tail of a French-built Concorde bearing the insignia of Air France, 1975.

THE PLATE
DESCRIPTIONS

1. Wright Flyer

Aviation history does not tell us much about John T. Daniels, except that he was a lifeguard from the Kill Devil Life Saving Station near Kitty Hawk, North Carolina; but he was the only one of the five spectators present on the morning of 17 December 1903 with the presence of mind to bring along a camera. The press, though invited, had disdained to attend, and Daniels, with two colleagues, was there ostensibly to give assistance in case of an accident; but without him the world would have had no photographic record of the birth of powered aeroplane flight.

The Wrights' latent interest in flight, dating perhaps from the gift of a toy helicopter in their youth, was awakened in 1896 by the death of Otto Lilienthal, the German gliding pioneer. 'It seemed to my brother and myself,' said Wilbur in 1901, 'that the main reason why the problem (of flight) had remained so long unsolved was that no one had

been able to obtain any adequate practice.' By then, no one could accuse Orville and Wilbur Wright of such a failing. Building their first aeroplane, a biplane kite, in August 1899, they progressed from this to three gliders in which they made about a dozen flights in 1900, about 700 in the following year, and upward of 1,400 in 1902. In 1901 they devised and built their own wind tunnel, using it to test more than 200 small surfaces – flat, concave, convex, square, oblong. From the results they developed the wing shape and construction for their third glider in 1902. All three gliders were manoeuvred in the air by warping, or twisting, the trailing-edges of the four wingtips – one pair upward, one pair downward – and when this system was linked to a movable rudder, on the third glider, they had mastered the basic problem of control in the air.

All that was needed now was an engine. This, too, they were obliged to produce for themselves, but at last, on 12

December 1903, they were ready for their first attempt at powered flight – only to find that the wind had dropped. Two days later there was enough wind for an attempt to be made. They flipped a coin, Wilbur winning the toss to decide who should be the pilot, but after about 100 ft. (30 m.) of a shaky take-off run Wilbur over-corrected the elevator and the aircraft, dubbed *Flyer*, suddenly settled heavily, breaking one of the propeller shafts. On 16 December, rain prevented the repaired machine from being brought out. The following morning dawned ice-cold, with a gusty 24 m.p.h. (39 km/hr.) wind, but at 10.35 a.m. local time Orville made a successful first take-off; and as it left the end of its launching rail, John Daniels' camera recorded the historic moment for all time. Orville's first flight, lasting 12 seconds, was followed by three more that morning: 11 seconds (Wilbur), 15 seconds (Orville) and 59 seconds (Wilbur). Seldom can a single minute in the history of mankind have been so full of significance for the future. Details of the various Wright Flyers can be found in *Pioneer Aircraft 1903–14*.

The Flyer III, chosen for illustration, was the first fully practical machine, and the one which the Wrights themselves considered their best. In present-day terms, it was what we might call the 'pre-production' Flyer, following the 'prototype' Flyers I and II, and led directly to the first 'production' version, the Wright Model A, which was supplied to the U.S. Army and was built under licence in Europe. In 1950, the Flyer III was restored and placed on permanent display at Carillon Park, Dayton, Ohio; the original Flyer I is preserved in the National Air and Space Museum of the Smithsonian Institution in Washington, D.C., and a replica of it in the Aeronautical Gallery of the Science Museum in London.

Specification of Wright Flyer III

Engine: One 15–20 h.p. Wright water-cooled in-line.
Span: 40 ft. 6 in. (12·34 m.).
Length: 28 ft. 0 in. (8·53 m.).
Height: approx. 8 ft. 0 in. (2·44 m.).
Wing area: 503·0 sq. ft. (46·73 sq. m.).
Take-off weight: approx. 930 lb. (422 kg.).
Speed: approx. 35 m.p.h. (56 km/hr.).

2. Blériot Type XI

In its issue of 5 October 1908, the London *Daily Mail* offered a prize of £1,000 for the first aeroplane crossing of the English Channel. Stipulations were that the flight must be made between dawn and dusk; that no part of the aircraft must touch the water en route; that the aircraft must not be sustained partly or wholly by a lighter-than-air gas; and that contestants must furnish witnessed statements of their points of departure and arrival.

The aeroplane with which Louis Blériot was to win that prize was completed some two months later, and made its first flight on 23 January 1909, powered by a 30 h.p. R.E.P. engine driving a four-blade propeller. Early flights proving disappointing, Blériot improved it during April and May by fitting a new engine and two-blade propeller; removing the over-fuselage fin; enlarging the rudder; increasing the wing span and area, and modifying the pivoting tips of the horizontal tail (elevons). Blériot's great rival for the Channel attempt, Hubert Latham, left Sangatte, near Calais, on 19 July 1909 in his Antoinette IV monoplane, but came down in the water some 7 miles (11 km) out after his engine failed.

On Sunday, 25 July, Blériot was awakened at dawn. The weather was favourable, and at 04.35 hours he took off from the field at Les Baraques, also near Calais. 'Where is Dover?' he had asked his friend Leblanc. 'Over there', came the reply, accompanied by a vague wave of the arm. Blériot's aircraft had no compass, but for the first 10 minutes he was able to follow the torpedo-boat *Escopette*, which was monitoring the flight in case of accidents. After overtaking the ship, Blériot was without sight of land for a further 10 minutes. When he did pick out the English coast, he found he had drifted eastwards to St. Margaret's Bay, and had to turn back towards Dover, where he landed in Northfall Meadow (near Dover Castle) at 05.12 hours.

First to greet him were a local policeman, a French reporter and a British Customs officer. After satisfying this last individual that his 'vessel' had no contraband or infectious diseases on board, Blériot was presented with his customs and immigration certificate and officially 'allowed' into the country. Presentation of his £1,000 prize, and a silver trophy, was made on the following day in London, while the aircraft went on public display in Selfridge's Oxford Street store. During the four days it was on show, it was seen by an estimated 120,000 people.

Blériot returned by ship to Paris, and even greater acclaim, on 28 July; the aircraft, on its return, was sold for 10,000 francs (about £400) to the French newspaper *Matin* for exhibition. It was subsequently presented to the Conservatoire des Arts et Métiers in Paris, where it remains to this day. Two days after Blériot's flight, Latham made a second attempt, in the Antoinette VII, this time getting to within a mile of Dover before again suffering an engine failure and having to ditch. Just under a year after Blériot's great flight, on 2 June 1910, a French-built Wright biplane, flown by the Hon. Charles Rolls, made the first double crossing of the Channel by aeroplane.

3. Henry Farman III

Just as the Blériot XI represented the archetypal European monoplane, it was the Voisin – a pusher-engined boxkite-wing machine with a biplane tail – that established the first classic biplane type to be built on the Continent, and by the summer of 1909 the Voisin brothers had produced nearly twenty for various customers. One of those customers was Henry Farman, who ordered one in June 1907 and by the end of the year had become the first person to remain airborne for more than a minute, and the first to fly more than a kilometre, on other than a Wright aircraft. During the next year and a half Farman was to introduce a number of innovations to what was otherwise a somewhat pedestrian design, turning it into one of the most practical and successful early European aircraft.

His first and major step, in late 1908, was to fit the first practical ailerons seen in Europe, so making the aircraft more efficient and more controllable.

Specification of Blériot XI
Engine: One 25 h.p. Anzani air-cooled semi-radial.
Span: 25 ft. 7⅛ in. (7·80 m.).
Length: 26 ft. 3 in. (8·00 m.).
Wing area: 150·7 sq. ft. (14·00 sq. m.).
Take-off weight: 661 lb. (300 kg.).
Speed: approx. 38 m.p.h. (61 km/hr.) on Channel crossing.

When, in 1908, another Voisin ordered by Farman was sold instead to a British buyer, Farman was so incensed that he cancelled his order and instead set up an aeroplane factory of his own. Its first product was the 1909 Farman III, which in developed form departed from the earlier Voisin design in having ailerons, no side-curtains between the wings, an open biplane tail with twin rudders behind it, and (eventually) one of the new 50 h.p. Gnome rotary engines. In this form, at the famous Reims meeting in August 1909, it won prizes for distance (112 miles; 180 km), altitude and passenger-carrying. This successful formula was to stay in production for two years with only detail improvements.

Two Farmans in particular which made the headlines in 1910 were those flown by Claude Grahame-White and Louis Paulhan in a bid for the £10,000 prize offered by the *Daily Mail* newspaper for the first flight between London and Manchester. The more experienced Paulhan, who left Hendon at 5.21 p.m. on 27 April and reached Manchester at 5.32 a.m. the following day, with only a single overnight stop, at Lichfield, was comfortably the winner. Grahame-White, who de-parted from Wormwood Scrubs at 6.29 p.m., made two stops (at Roade and Polesworth), and was still 4 miles (6·4 km) short of Lichfield as Paulhan touched down at Manchester; but gained almost equal distinction for having made one of the first-ever night flights in an attempt to overtake his rival. When the *Mail*'s prize was first offered, its great rival, the *Daily Sketch*, derisively offered £10 million for the first flying machine of any kind to fly 5 miles (8 km) from London and back again. One is tempted to suggest that someone should have taken the *Sketch* at its word; though Paulhan is reputed to have said that he would not repeat his experience 'for ten thousand times ten thousand pounds'.

**Specification of
Henry Farman III**

Engine: One 50 h.p. Gnome rotary.
Span: 32 ft. 9¾ in. (10·00 m.).
Length: 39 ft. 4½ in. (12·00 m.).
Wing area: 430·6 sq. ft. (40·00 sq. m.).
Take-off weight: 1,213 lb. (550 kg.).
Maximum speed: 37 m.p.h. (60 km/hr.).
Aircraft flown by Paulhan had upper wing span increased to 34 ft. 1½ in. (10·40 m.).

---

4. Curtiss Hydro-aeroplane

No one can take from French-man Henri Fabre the distinction of being the first man to take off from water in a powered aero-plane, but Fabre himself would probably have been the last to claim that his 1910 Hydravion was in any way a practical flying machine. The great pioneer of waterborne flight was the Ameri-can Glenn Hammond Curtiss who, in May 1910 (only a few weeks after Fabre's first efforts), made a flight down the Hudson River from Albany to New York. Under the lower wings, though happily not needed on this occa-sion, were two cylindrical metal tanks intended to provide flota-tion if a forced landing on the water proved necessary. Well before this Curtiss had already tried to interest the U.S. Navy in developing waterborne aircraft, but was told in August 1909 that 'the Department does not con-sider that the development of an aeroplane has progressed suffi-ciently at this time for use in the Navy'. However, in late 1910 it attached Captain Washington Irving Chambers to keep an eye on aviation progress 'with a view to advising the Department con-cerning the adaptability of such material for naval use'.

That autumn, Curtiss had set up a test of one of his standard 'Golden Flyer' biplanes, flown by his friend John McCurdy, to be flown off a special platform on the deck of the Hamburg–Ameri-can steamship *Pennsylvania*, but the trial had had to be cancelled. Hearing of this the U.S. Navy offered the cruiser *Birmingham* for a similar trial, and on 14 November 1910, at Hampton Roads, Virginia, Eugene Ely made a successful take-off. A landing-on trial, also successful, was made by Ely on 18 January 1911; the location this time was San Francisco Bay and the ship a U.S. battleship, also, coinci-dentally, named *Pennsylvania*.

So far, so good; but these trials had been conducted with land-planes. What the U.S. Navy wanted was a seaplane, and Curtiss's first experiment of this kind in 1908, somewhat aptly named the Loon, had been a failure. Now, however, he pro-duced his second attempt, basic-ally a standard 'Golden Flyer' mounted on a single, nearly-square Fabre-type float, with a smaller float of similar shape in place of the nosewheel. Curtiss himself was the pilot when, on 26 January 1911, it made a success-ful take-off. This hydro-aero-plane, as it was known, then underwent several development stages. The two original floats were replaced by a longer single one; the seat was then placed aft of the engine and the propeller moved to the front; later still, the propeller was restored to its original 'pusher' position. In February 1911 wheels were added to make it the world's first amphibious aircraft; these, later still, were made retractable; and for a brief period it carried triplane wings. In the wheel/float biplane form, it achieved the success that Curtiss sought, and in May 1911 the Navy ordered two examples – one landplane, and one amphibian. Thus encouraged, Curtiss continued his pioneering of marine aircraft, marking up another milestone on 10 January 1912 with the flight of the world's first flying-boat. Exactly two years later, his foresight and determination were acknowledged publicly when a Navy Department press release declared that '... the science of aerial navigation has reached that point where aircraft must form a large part of our naval force for offensive and defensive operations'.

5. Avro 504

On the page from an exercise book on which his first rough sketches for the 504 were made, a plan view of the cockpit is annotated in A. V. Roe's hand '20 inches should be enough for broadest of shoulders, but just measure some big 'uns and see'. Such were the refinements of aeroplane design in 1913. In a later comment, Roe recorded that 'when I designed this aeroplane I thought that we would be fortunate if we received an order for half a dozen'. In fact, his factories and others were fortunate to the tune of well over ten thousand 504s, nearly 80 per cent of them during World War I and the remainder over a period extending up to 1931.

Construction of the prototype 504 was begun at Brooklands in

Specification of Curtiss Hydro-aeroplane

Data apply to A-1 Triad.
Engine: One 75 h.p. Curtiss Vee-type.
Span over ailerons: 37 ft. 2 in. (11·33 m.).
Length: 28 ft. 7⅛ in. (8·72 m.).
Wing area: 286·0 sq. ft. (26·57 sq. m.).
Take-off weight: 1,575 lb. (714·5 kg.).
Maximum speed: 60 m.p.h. (96·5 km/hr.).

April 1913, where it made its first flight three months later, piloted by F. P. Raynham. Its public début, as an entrant in the second U.K. Aerial Derby, followed on 20 September 1913. Success in this event was denied it (it came fourth), but its appearance and handling qualities attracted much favourable comment, and on 10 February 1914 Raynham flew it to a height of 14,420 ft. (4,395 m.) to set an unofficial British altitude record. Shortly after this the prototype was purchased by the *Daily Mail* newspaper, for whom Raynham took it on a tour of British coastal resorts later in the year, giving passenger flights at £5 a time.

To interchange with the normal land undercarriage a float landing gear (as illustrated) was provided; the first flight with this gear was made at Paignton in April 1914. Sadly, this historic aeroplane survived the outbreak of war by only two days: on 6 August 1914, when taking off for a delivery flight to the British Services, the wretched Monosoupape engine failed, and the ensuing crash damaged it beyond repair. More than 8,300 other Avro 504s did participate in the war, however, as day and night fighters, anti-Zeppelin

fighters and bombers with the R.F.C. and R.N.A.S. – but above all as trainers. At the School of Special Flying, formed at Gosport in 1917 under Major R. R. Smith-Barry, the Avro was 'wrung out' by instructors and pupil pilots during the ensuing years to a degree never dreamt of by its designer, and played a major part in establishing a pattern of safe and effective flying training that endured for decades. The brunt of this work was borne by the 504J 'Mono Avro', the 504K 'Standard Avro' and the 504N 'Lynx Avro'. With more than 270 'demobbed' Avro 504Ks giving training or joyriding thrills to the general public throughout the 1920s, they rivalled the ubiquitous de Havilland Moth in popular appeal. Alliott Verdon Roe certainly got that 1913 design right: as an-

---

Specification of Avro 504
Engine: One 80 h.p. Gnome Monosoupape rotary.
Span: 36 ft. 0 in. (10·97 m.).
Length (landplane): 29 ft. 3 in. (8·91 m.).
Wing area: 342·0 sq. ft. (31·77 sq. m.).
Take-off weight (landplane): 1,550 lb. (703 kg.).
Maximum speed (landplane): 81 m.p.h. (130 km/hr.).

---

other and more eloquent historian has justly claimed, the Avro 504 exhibited 'that rare symmetry and balance of areas that distinguished it as the great aeroplane it truly was'.

6. Caproni bomber

The name of Count Giovanni Caproni di Taliedo is rightly an honoured one in the history of aviation. One of his little biplanes still holds the world altitude record for piston-engined aircraft, set in 1938, and he shares with Igor Sikorsky the distinction of producing the first multi-engined heavy bombers to go into operational service. Italy, in its 1911 war with Turkey, was the first nation to drop bombs from an aeroplane in anger, and some two years later Caproni completed the design of a large three-engined biplane bomber. After some revision to improve the power installation, a prototype was flown in October 1914, and in the following June the Italian Army cautiously placed an order for twelve bombers, designated Ca 1 and powered by three 100 h.p. Fiat A.10 engines.

On 20 August 1915 a raid by two of them on the town of Aisovizza marked the Ca 1's operational début; within the next eighteen months no fewer than fourteen Italian squadrons were equipped with Capronis, and by the end of the war this total had exceeded twenty. Many different variants appeared – so many that in later years a whole string of manufacturer's designations were coined to identify them – but the three major types bore the Italian Army designations Ca 1, Ca 3 and Ca 5. (A further series, the Ca 4s, were much larger and of triplane configuration.) Probably the greatest of their attributes were their dependability and survivability: they were frequently called upon to make long-distance flights across the Alps in winter, and their capacity for absorbing battle damage was considerable.

The first award of Italy's counterpart to the Victoria Cross went to Captain Oreste Salomone, who on 18 February 1916 brought back to base a dead crew in a much-crippled Ca 1 after a raid on Ljubljana. Many other medals were deserved, if not actually received, by the gunners who endured flight after flight in their open, cage-like positions just aft of the upper wing and directly above the pusher propeller. The Ca 5, which entered service in early 1918, was a more powerful development (three 200 h.p. instead of 150 h.p. engines), but the brunt of wartime operations was borne by the Ca 3, including, from January 1917, bombing missions by night as well as by day. A modified version of the Ca 3 was put back into production in 1923, the Regia Aeronautica receiving 144 which were mostly used in North Africa in Italy's campaign to 'restore' her 'lost colonies'. Only one Caproni bomber is known to survive: a Ca 3, preserved in the Museo Nazionale della Scienza e della Tecnica in Milan.

Specification of Caproni Ca 5

Engines: Three 200 h.p. Fiat A. 12*bis* in-lines.
Span: 76 ft. 9¼ in. (23·40 m.).
Length: 41 ft. 4⅞ in. (12·62 m.).
Wing area: 1,614·6 sq. ft. (150·00 sq. m.).
Take-off weight: 11,685 lb. (5,300 kg.).
Maximum speed: 94 m.p.h. (152 km/hr.) at sea level.
Service ceiling: 14,765 ft. (4,500 m.).
Endurance: 4 hr. 0 min.

---

7.   de Havilland D.H.2

Historians may dispute the right of the D.H.2 to be called one of the 'famous aircraft of all time',

but in many respects it was the best of the British fighters available in 1916 to combat the menace of the synchronised, front-gunned Fokker Eindeckers. One Victoria Cross was earned in it, another holder of the V.C. died in it, and among its early pilots was one Flight Sergeant J. T. B. McCudden, later (and on better aircraft) to become one of the leading British fighter aces of World War 1. The V.C. went to Major L. W. B. Rees, C.O. of No. 32 Squadron, for an action in July 1916 in which he attacked, single-handed, a formation of ten German two-seaters en route to bomb a British target. Rees forced down two of the enemy, and caused the remainder to break up and abandon their raid. The V.C. who died was Major Lanoe G. Hawker, C.O. of No. 24 Squadron, who on 23 November 1916 fell victim to an Albatros D.II flown by the legendary Manfred von Richthofen.

Relatively clean-lined for a pusher biplane, the D.H.2 was in essence a scaled-down single-seat development of de Havilland's earlier D.H.1/1A. Its armament, a single Lewis machine-gun, was installed in the nose, on a none-too-steady mounting; in practice, many pilots disregarded instructions and 'fixed' it in the dead-ahead position with some form of clip, so aiming their aircraft at the enemy in order to aim the gun. The D.H.2 had light, sensitive controls, and was only half the weight of its Fokker-fighting contemporary, the F.E. 2b; and its biplane configuration gave it a wing loading of about 5·8 lb/sq. ft. (28·3 kg/sq. m.) compared with a figure of more than 8 for the monoplane Fokker. It was faster than the Fokker, and had a better rate of climb (6,000 ft.; 1,830 m. in 11 minutes). What it lacked in effective firepower it made up for in ruggedness and manoeuvrability, fulfilling the principle that 'thrice blessed is he who gets his blow in first'. Delivered to

---

Specification of de Havilland D.H.2

Engine: One 100 h.p. Gnome Monosoupape rotary.
Span: 28 ft. 3 in. (8·61 m.).
Length: 25 ft. 2½ in. (7·68 m.).
Wing area: 249·0 sq. ft. (23·13 sq. m.).
Take-off weight: 1,441 lb. (654 kg.).
Maximum speed: 93 m.p.h. (150 km/hr.) at sea level.
Service ceiling: 14,500 ft. (4,420 m.).
Endurance: 2 hr. 45 min.

Western Front squadrons of the R.F.C. from January 1916, it remained effective until the following autumn before the new generation of German biplane fighters began to outclass it, and itself began to be replaced in the following spring.

8. Fokker Eindecker

If French pilot Roland Garros had not been shot down near Courtrai on 19 April 1915, or if he had been luckier in his attempts to destroy his aircraft, the world would probably have heard little of the Fokker Eindecker, for it was then in service only in small numbers as a fast communications aircraft. But, with the capture of Garros' special Morane–Saulnier Type L parasol monoplane, Germany gained possession of the first device to be used in air combat that enabled a machine-gun to fire through plates and to deflect those bullets which struck the blades; but Luebbe, Heber and Leimberger, three of Fokker's engineers at Schwerin, went one better. Adopting, in essence, the principle of 'letting the propeller fire the gun', they came up with a mechanical 'interrupter' gear which adjusted the rate of fire to the propeller's rate of turn, i.e.

firing was interrupted as a blade passed in front of the gun.

In the hands of such leading pilots as Oswald Boelcke, Max Immelmann and others, the Fokker soon became a formidable fighting machine, successes mounting as the number of aircraft in service increased. The hastily-produced E.I was quickly followed by the E.II with powerplant and other improvements, and by the principal service version, the E.III. The first recorded Eindecker victim, probably a B.E.2, fell near Douai on 1 August 1915 to one of the prototype aircraft flown by Immelmann. In October the so-called 'Fokker scourge' began in earnest, and throughout the ensuing winter, against negligible Allied opposition, they gained a reputation for deadliness far in excess of their true military value. Many of their victims were variants of the two-seat B.E.2, an otherwise worthy aeroplane that just did not have the speed or agility to get out of their way. But in January and February 1916 Allied squadrons in France began to re-equip in strength with D.H.2, F.E.2b and Nieuport 11 fighters, and the decline of the Fokkers' reign of supremacy began.

The E.III illustrated is the only genuine example of its kind still known to exist, though one has been reported in East Germany.

Specification of Fokker E. III
Engine: One 100 h.p. Oberursel U.I rotary. *Span:* 31 ft. 2¾ in. (9·52 m.). *Length:* 23 ft. 11⅓ in. (7·30 m.). *Wing area:* approx. 172·2 sq. ft. (16·00 sq. m.). *Take-off weight:* 1,400 lb. (635 kg.). *Maximum speed:* 83 m.p.h. (134 km/hr.) at 6,500 ft. (1,980 m.). *Service ceiling:* 11,500 ft. (3,500 m.). *Endurance:* 2 hr. 45 min.

9. Spad VII

That the Spad VII was the first really good fighting machine to emerge from the Spad company can be attributed not only to its designer, Louis Béchereau, but to the happy circumstance that the right engine also came along at the right time. This, the Hispano-Suiza water-cooled Vee engine designed by Swiss engineer Marc Birkigt, could be ranked with the Rolls-Royces and Napiers of its day, and came just as the widely-used rotaries were at the virtual limit of their development. First flown in April 1916, the Spad VII not only possessed excellent handling qualities but was also a strong and stable gun platform. Nearly 6,000 were built, and served with the air forces of Belgium, France, Great Britain, Italy, Russia and the United States.

The Spad VII was flown by many great and successful pilots of World War 1, but is probably associated most with Capitaine Georges Guynemer, second only to René Fonck as France's top-scoring pilot, with fifty-four victories to his credit. Guynemer called the Spad VII his 'mitrailleuse volante' (flying machine-gun) – as well he might, since it brought him some 60 per cent of all his victories in a period of less than a year. He already had fourteen enemy scalps to his credit, flying the Morane Parasol and Nicuport scout, before picking up his first Spad victim in mid-September 1916. By the end of the following June he had increased that total to forty-eight.

Guynemer was also the inspiration behind the Spad XII, virtually a VII fitted with a 200 h.p. Hispano-Suiza having a single-shot 37-mm. cannon mounted between the cylinder banks, and this brought him a

further four victories in the summer of 1917. By this time the newer Spad XIII was being introduced into service, and it was in one of these that the French hero was to lose his life on 11 September 1917, when only a few weeks short of his 23rd birthday. The circumstances of his death – missing on a flight over Belgium – remained a mystery for many years, but it now seems most likely that he fell victim to the guns of a Rumpler two-seater.

Specification of Spad VII
Engine: One 150 h.p.
Hispano-Suiza 8 Aa Vee-type.
Span: 25 ft. 8 in. (7·82 m.).
Length: 20 ft. 3½ in. (6·18 m.).
Wing area: 193·75 sq. ft.
(18·00 sq. m.).
Take-off weight: 1,554 lb. (705 kg.).
Maximum speed: 114 m.p.h.
(183 km/hr.) at 6,560 ft.
(2,000 m.).
Service ceiling: 18,050 ft.
(5,500 m.).
Endurance: 2 hr. 40 min.

---

10. Albatros D.III

Middle member of the Albatros family of D-type single-seat fighters, the D.III was undoubtedly the best of a good bunch. From mid-1916, first the D.I and then the D.II had begun successfully to wrest back the air supremacy over the Western Front which French and British squadrons had regained at some effort from the Fokker monoplane. One of Britain's leading D.H.2 pilots, Major Lanoe Hawker, succumbed to a D.II flown by Manfred von Richthofen, and other leading lights of the German Air Service – among them Boelcke, Udet and Voss – also played a part in making the presence of the Albatros felt.

Compared with the early versions, the D.III exhibited a number of design changes, of which the narrower-chord lower wings and interplane V struts were no doubt the result of studying captured Nieuport scouts. The Albatros D.III was a handsome machine, with an excellently streamlined bullet-shaped body neatly capped by the large propeller spinner. It was also very strongly built: it had a two-spar upper wing and the fuselage structure consisted of six longerons, oval former frames and a plywood skin. With its forward-firing two-gun armament, and high speed, it represented a marked improvement over the slower, more fragile and usually single-gunned Fokker E.III.

Its heyday was in the first half of 1917, including a particularly successful period in 'Bloody April' during which a heavy toll was exacted of Allied aircraft – mostly the luckless B.E.2c. The subject of the illustration is one of the Series 153 Albatros D.IIIs, built for the Austro-Hungarian Fliegertruppe by Oeffag and flown by that country's most successful fighter pilot, Hauptmann Godwin Brumowski. This officer had, by the time of the Armistice, accumulated thirty-eight certain victories and three 'probables', and numbered the Iron Cross and the Order of Leopold among his many decorations. The Albatros D.V. and

Specification of Albatros D.III

Engine: One 200 h.p. Austro-Daimler in-line.
Span: 29 ft. 8⅛ in. (9·05 m.).
Length: 24 ft. 0⅝ in. (7·33 m.).
Wing area: 220·7 sq. ft. (20·50 sq. m.).
Take-off weight: 1,953 lb. (886 kg.).
Maximum speed: 102·5 m.p.h. (165 km/hr.) at 3,280 ft. (1,000 m.).
Service ceiling: 18,050 ft. (5,500 m.).
Endurance: 2 hr. 0 min.

D.Va, which followed the D.III, did not achieve the degree of improved performance expected, although they were equally successful and more widely used. However, two D.Vs, one in Canberra and one in Washington, represent the only examples of the Albatros D types still in being today.

11. Nieuport 17

Despite a tendency for its narrow, single-spar lower wings to twist when diving or turning under pronounced stress, the Nieuport 17 was by no means as frail as its appearance suggested. Indeed it is highly likely that it was placed more often into such a stress situation by its pilots simply because of its considerable ability to manoeuvre tightly; certainly there was no shortage of expert fliers at hand to put the little French fighter through its paces. The list of their names reads like a roll of honour in itself: Boyau, Dorne, Duellin, Guérin, Guynemer, Navarre, Nungesser and Pinsard of France; de Meulemeester, Jaquet, Olieslagers and Thieffry of Belgium; Baracca and Scaroni of Italy; Ball and Bishop of the Royal Flying Corps; and many

more. The much wounded Nungesser, whose Nie. 17C.1 is illustrated, scored a major proportion of his forty-five wartime victories in this machine and, later, in the more streamlined Nieuport 24 bis. It was a sad day for aviation when, with François Coli, he was lost during an attempted transatlantic flight in May 1927.

Secrets of the Nieuport's success as a dog-fighter were its speed – its predecessor, the Nie. 11, had originated in a design for the Gordon Bennett Trophy; its great manoeuvrability – due, among other reasons, to the close grouping of all the principal heavy components around its major axis; and its climbing ability. Commander Samson of the Royal Naval Air Service once said of the Nie. 17 that it climbed 'like a witch', and a measure of this statement is that it could get up to 10,000 ft. (3,050 m.) in about 10 minutes. By comparison, even the Albatros D.III, a later design, took some $12\frac{1}{4}$ minutes to reach a comparable altitude; its predecessor, the Fokker E.III, needed 28 minutes; the D.H.2, depending upon the engine fitted, could do it in some 25–31 minutes; while the poor F.E.2b required almost 40 minutes to achieve this relatively modest altitude. One Nie. 11 survives in Brussels, and one Nie. 17 in Paris.

Specification of Nieuport 17
Engine: One 110 h.p. Le Rhône 9 J rotary.
Span: 26 ft. 11⅝ in. (8·22 m.).
Length: 18 ft. 10 in. (5·74 m.).
Wing area: 161·5 sq. ft. (15·00 sq. m.).
Take-off weight: 1,246 lb. (565 kg.).
Maximum speed: 110 m.p.h. (177 km/hr.) at 6,560 ft. (2,000 m.).
Service ceiling: 17,390 ft. (5,300 m.).
Endurance: 2 hr. 0 min.

---

12.   de Havilland D.H.9A

The first British aeroplane to be designed from the outset as a day bomber was the de Havilland D.H.4, which made its first flight in August 1916 and served in substantial numbers from early 1917 until the end of World War I. Its replacement by the D.H.9, told in more detail in *Bombers 1914–1919*, was a retrograde step, stemming principally from the variety of unsatisfactory engines that were installed in it. Trenchard wanted its production cancelled, but was too late to do

so, and more than 4,000 found their way into RFC/RNAS/RAF service. With the advent of the American Liberty 12 engine in 1918, however, the basic airframe design was vindicated and, as the D.H.9A, became one of the most respected and trustworthy aircraft of the Royal Air Force. Its wartime service was limited – deliveries did not begin until June 1918 – but two squadrons served as bombers with Trenchard's Independent Force.

It was in post-war service, however, that the 'Ninak' established its reputation. It became involved in the 1919–20 war by the White Russians against the Bolsheviks (who paid it the compliment of building a copied version), and from then until the end of the decade was involved in a whole series of 'other people's wars'. It was involved in the Afghan war in India which began in 1919; a decade of conflict in Mesopotamia/Iraq; it fought the Turks at Constantinople in 1922, and the Arabs in Palestine from 1924. Apart from its normal day-bomber duties, it carried stretcher patients, aerial surveyors, and a fair amount of the Cairo–Baghdad air mail. In India, in 1928–29, it flew escort in appalling blizzards to the R.A.F. transports used in the evacuation of Kabul. Universally reliable in Arctic, temperate or tropical climates, it earned a high reputation and considerable respect from friend and foe alike, and was one of the standard workhorses of the Royal Air Force until as late as 1931. Surviving examples exist in Paris, Krakow and Johannesburg.

**Specification of
de Havilland D.H.9A**

Engine: One 400 h.p. Liberty 12 Vee-type.
Span: 45 ft. 11⅜ in. (14·00 m.).
Length: 30 ft. 3 in. (9·22 m.).
Wing area: 486·7 sq. ft. (45·22 sq. m.).
Maximum take-off weight: 4,220 lb. (1,914 kg.).
Maximum speed: 120 m.p.h. (193 km/hr.) at 10,000 ft. (3,050 m.).
Service ceiling: 19,000 ft. (5,790 m.).
Normal endurance: 5 hr. 45 min.

---

13. Bristol Fighter

Known as the 'Biff' during World War 1, as the 'Brisfit' later, and more formally throughout its long service life as the F.2B, the Bristol Fighter was one of the classic aeroplanes of its time. Born as a two-seat reconnaissance aircraft, it became a fighter when allied with the Rolls-Royce Falcon engine, and carried out its first operational duties in April 1917. A year later, at dawn on 1 April 1918, Bristol Fighters of No. 22 Squadron carried out the first official duties of the newly-created Royal Air Force. Combat losses were considerable at first, mainly due to squadrons adopting 'two-seat tactics' against the enemy; but, when flown as though it were a single-seat fighter (with an effective sting in its tail), it soon came to be a highly-respected opponent in the skies over France, and was probably the finest aircraft in the two-seat class to be used during the war.

Strangely, efforts to emulate the D.H.4, by producing an American version fitted with the Liberty engine (which was unsuitable for the Bristol anyway), were further confounded by ill-advised and mishandled attempts to redesign the airframe for American production, with the result that Curtiss built only twenty-seven of the 2,000 planned and the F.2B gained a thoroughly bad but undeserved reputation in the U.S.A. With the R.A.F., however, it continued to improve even upon the affection in which it had been held in 1917–18.

With the D.H.9A, it was one of the two principal maids-of-all-work throughout the 1920s, serving in the U.K., China, Egypt, Germany, India, Iraq, Palestine and Turkey, in a variety of roles that included fighting, bombing, Army co-operation and photo-reconnaissance among many others. It was particularly active in the third Afghan war on the North-West Frontier in India, and in the campaign against Sheikh Mahmoud in Kurdistan and Mustafa Kemal in Turkey; and, with the

R.A.F. very much on the thin end of a meagre defence budget, the lack of spares, maintenance facilities and reinforcements demanded a high rate of utilisation and dependability. The Brisfit was equal to the task, and did not disappear from R.A.F. first-line squadrons until 1932. Examples survive in Britain, in the Imperial War Museum and, in flying condition, in the Shuttleworth Collection.

14. Fokker Triplane

The Fokker triplane – or Dr. I (Dreidecker Type I) to give it its more formal designation – was not, as is often said or implied, a 'copy' of the Sopwith triplane which had gone into action with the British air services at the end of 1916. But it was, indisputably, an outcome of the effect which the introduction of the British type had had upon the air fighting over the Western Front; indeed, German and Austro-Hungarian companies had such an attack of 'triplanitis' that no fewer than fourteen of them had produced triple-winged fighter designs by the end of 1917.

First and most successful was the Fokker machine, designed in

---

Specification of Bristol Fighter

Engine: One 275 h.p. Rolls-Royce Falcon III Vee-type.
Span: 39 ft. 3 in. (11·96 m.).
Length: 25 ft. 10 in. (7·87 m.).
Wing area: 405·6 sq. ft. (37·68 sq. m.).
Take-off weight: 2,779 lb. (1,261 kg.).
Maximum speed: 119 m.p.h. (191·5 km/hr.) at 6,500 ft. (1,980 m.).
Service ceiling: 20,000 ft. (6,100 m.).
Endurance: 3 hr. 0 min.

---

the late spring of that year by the brilliant Reinhold Platz and carrying out its first operations with von Richthofen's Jagdgeschwader I in August. These were performed by the second and third prototypes, the latter being almost exclusively the mount of Leutnant Werner Voss, one of Germany's leading fighter pilots. Voss scored his first victory in the Dr. I on 30 August, and went on to score a further twenty in the next three weeks before, on 23 September, he was shot down and killed by an S.E.5a of No. 56 Squadron, R.F.C. The second prototype had an even shorter operational life, beginning on 1 September when flown by Manfred von Richthofen in the course of scoring his 60th victory of the war, and ending only a fortnight later when shot down by Sopwith Camels of No. 10 Squadron R.N.A.S., the German pilot on that day being Oblt Kurt Wolff of Jasta 11.

Despite these early casualties the Fokker triplane was warmly welcomed by its crews, and would not have gone so early to so eminent a unit as JG I if it had not been so good. Main production deliveries began in October 1917, and the triplane was fully operational by the end of the year, providing pilots of Albatros and Pfalz fighters with a mount that could put them on terms with the S.E.5a, Bristol Fighter and Spad, thanks to its first-class manoeuvrability and a rate of climb that could take it to 13,125 ft. (4,000 m.) in 15 minutes or less. One often sees reference to 'Richthofen's triplane' as though to suggest that this was a single aircraft. In fact, the Rittmeister flew several, and became its greatest exponent before his death on 21 April 1918 in the example illustrated. Other famous exponents of the little Fokker included his brother Lothar, Ernst Udet and Hermann Göring.

Specification of Fokker Triplane
Engine: One 110 h.p. Oberursel UR.II rotary.
Span: 23 ft. 7⅝ in. (7·19 m.).
Length: 18 ft. 11⅛ in. (5·77 m.).
Wing area: 200·9 sq. ft. (18·66 sq. m.).
Take-off weight: 1,290 lb. (585 kg.).
Maximum speed: 102·5 m.p.h. (165 km/hr.) at 13,125 ft. (4,000 m.).
Service ceiling: 19,685 ft. (6,000 m.).
Endurance: 1 hr. 30 min.

15. Sopwith Camel

Famous descendant of the Tabloid, Baby, 1½-Strutter, Pup and Triplane, the Camel is deservedly remembered as the greatest progeny of Sopwith's outstanding chief designer, Herbert Smith. In only sixteen months of operational service, from May 1917 until the Armistice, it destroyed more enemy aircraft than any other single combat type during World War 1. Though controversy still continues over the degree to which the Camel flown by Captain Roy Brown of No. 209 Squadron was the direct cause of the death of Baron Manfred von Richthofen, there is no doubt that it was instrumental in bringing about the downfall of Germany's legendary airman. Less in dispute is the fact that a later-model Camel, a 2F.1 flown by Flt Sub-Lt Stuart Culley, shot down the last Zeppelin of the war, L53, on 11 August 1918. But it is not for its combat record alone that the Camel is remembered. It was Sopwith philosophy to give priority in design to handling qualities and view from the cockpit, which, in the Camel particularly, resulted in the grouping of engine, fuel, armament and pilot in as close an area as possible.

Unlike the Pup before it, and the Snipe which came after, the Camel was not a well-mannered aircraft to fly, and could be quite unforgiving to a careless or inexperienced pilot. The gyroscopic torque effect of some 350 lb. (158 kg.) of crankcase and cylinders spinning around the crankshaft at about 1,250 r.p.m. produced a manoeuvring response that, to say the least, was lively, and a sudden change of direction could – and did – often lead to a loss of rudder control and the onset of a fatal spin. In one pilot's view, the Camel offered its pilot one of three alternatives – 'Victoria Cross, Red Cross – or wooden cross'. But once the technique of flying it had been mastered, there was

---

Specification of Sopwith Camel

Engine: One 130 h.p. Clerget 9 B rotary.
Span: 28 ft. 0 in. (8·53 m.).
Length: 18 ft. 9 in. (5·72 m.).
Wing area: 231·0 sq. ft. (21·46 sq. m.).
Take-off weight: 1,453 lb. (659 kg.).
Maximum speed: 113 m.p.h. (182 km/hr.) at 10,000 ft. (3,050 m.).
Service ceiling: 19,000 ft. (5,790 m.).
Endurance: 2 hr. 30 min.

no better dogfighter to be found. Nearly 5,500 Camels were built, over half of which were still in service at the end of the war. Today only a handful survive, including two in the United Kingdom, two in the United States, and one each in Belgium, Canada and Poland.

16. Fokker D.VII

Unlike the Camel, the Fokker D.VII has been described as an extremely forgiving aeroplane to fly, and one capable of making a good pilot out of a novice. Of the thirty-one contenders in the fighter competition held at Adlershof in January 1918 (nine of which were Fokker designs), Fokker's V.11 prototype was so outstandingly a clear winner that an immediate contract was placed for 400 production aircraft – an unprecedented order, even at that late stage of the war. The first D.VII fighters began to be delivered in April 1918, and by the end of the war between 800–900 had entered service with nearly eighty Jagdstaffeln, about half of them built under licence by the Albatros and O.A.W. factories.

Apart from its excellent handling qualities, the D.VII was immensely strong, with two-spar upper and lower wings and a welded steel tube fuselage; its thick-section wings gave useful lift even in relatively thin air, thus maintaining its excellent performance at altitude; even the little aerofoil-type fairing over the main axle, a typical Fokker trademark, gave enough lift to offset the weight of the landing gear. With the 160 h.p. Mercedes D.III engine, for which it was designed, its performance was healthy enough, but this was improved immeasurably in the D.VII F by adopting the 185 h.p. B.M.W. IIIa, a first-class engine in which the decrease of power with altitude was considerably lower. Rated at 185 h.p. at sea level, it offered only 5 h.p. less at 6,000 ft. (1,830 m.), and was still good for 120 h.p. at 18,000 ft. (5,490 m.). What this meant in comparative rates of climb is graphically shown by the following comparative figures (see Table overleaf).

Such was its reputation that the D.VII was accorded the still-unique distinction of specific mention, by name, in Article IV of the Armistice Agreement, among equipment handed over to the Allies. Fokker, typically, had other ideas, and organised the escape into his native Holland of six train-loads comprising

	Mercedes	B.M.W.
Time to 1,000 m. (3,280 ft.)	4 min. 15 sec.	1 min. 45 sec.
„ „ 2,000 m. (6,560 ft.)	8 min. 18 sec.	4 min. 0 sec.
„ „ 3,000 m. (9,840 ft.)	13 min. 49 sec.	7 min. 0 sec.
„ „ 4,000 m. (13,120 ft.)	22 min. 48 sec.	10 min. 15 sec.
„ „ 5,000 m. (16,400 ft.)	38 min. 5 sec.	14 min. 0 sec.
„ „ 6,000 m. (19,680 ft.)	—	18 min. 45 sec.

some 220 airframes and more than 400 aircraft engines, among which were some 120 complete or near-complete examples of the D.VII – enough to resume post-war production and export of this remarkable aircraft. Today only a handful survive, including single examples in the R.A.F. Museum at Hendon, the Musée de l'Air in Paris, the Deutsches Museum in Munich, the National Aeronautical Collection of Can-ada, and the National Air and Space Museum in Washington.

17. Navy-Curtiss NC-TA

The quartet of NC (Navy-Curtiss) flying-boats were brought into being originally in response to a requirement issued on 25 August 1917 by Admiral David W. Taylor, Chief Constructor of the U.S. Navy, for a long-endurance aircraft capable of attacking German U-boats from the air. The contract for their completion was awarded in January 1918, and the first of them, NC-1, made its first flight on 4 October 1918.

With the war then virtually over, it was decided to use them for an attempt to fly across the North Atlantic in stages. A route via Newfoundland and the Azores was approved by the Secretary of the Navy, Josephus Daniels, on 4 February 1919, and preparations for the flight began under the direction of Com-

---

**Specification of
Fokker D.VII**

Engine: One 185 h.p. B.M.W.IIIa in-line.
Span: 29 ft. 2⅓ in. (8·90 m.).
Length: 22 ft. 9¾ in. (6·954 m.).
Wing area: 220·7 sq. ft. (20·50 sq. m.).
Take-off weight: 2,116 lb. (960 kg.).
Maximum speed: 124 m.p.h. (200 km/hr.) at 3,280 ft. (1,000 m.).
Service ceiling: 19,685 ft. (6,000 m.).
Endurance: 1 hr. 30 min.

mander John H. Towers. The second aircraft, NC-2, was withdrawn because of an unsatisfactory engine layout, but on 8 May 1919 Seaplane Division One, comprising NC-1, NC-3 and NC-4, left Naval Air Station Rockaway, on Long Island, on the 1,000 mile (1,610 km) trip to their starting-point at Trepassy Bay, Newfoundland. At about 6 p.m. on 16 May, the three flying-boats took off from Trepassy and headed for the Azores, commanded respectively by Towers (NC-1), Lt Cdr P. N. L. Bellinger (NC-3) and Lt Cdr Arthur C. Read (NC-4).

After more than 15 hours in the air, fog obliged both NC-1 and NC-3 to alight before reaching the Azores, both sustaining damage from the landing and from very heavy seas and being unable to take off again. NC-1 drifted and taxied its way into Ponta Delgada, where it arrived in the early evening of 19 May. Its sister boat, NC-3, was twice taken under tow, by a Greek steamer and a U.S. Navy vessel, but twice broke adrift and eventually sank, its crew being taken on to Horta by the steamer *Ionia*. Meanwhile, shortly after mid-day on 17 May, NC-4 had successfully completed its journey and landed at Horta. Its

crew, in addition to Lt Cdr Read, consisted of Lts E. F. Stone, W. K. Hinton and J. L. Breese, Ensign H. C. Rodd, and Chief Machinist's Mate E. S. Rhoads. NC-4 flew on to Ponta Delgada three days later, from where on 27 May it took off for the final transatlantic stage of the journey to Lisbon, arriving at one minute past eight that evening. Later, on 31 May, NC-4 continued its journey by flying to Plymouth, England, so completing 4,320 miles (6,952 km) in a flying time of 53 hours 58 minutes.

Eventually, after a triumphal return to the United States, it was handed over to the Smithsonian Institution in Washington, D.C., in whose National Air and Space Museum it still remains. Historians in later years have tended sometime to belittle the flight of the NC-4, on the grounds that it was not a non-stop flight like that made by Alcock and Brown only a few weeks later. This not only does a disservice to the achievements of an excellent aeroplane and a fine crew, but to the organisation behind the Atlantic flight. The non-stop crossing in the Vimy (see next entry) was an inspired flight by two courageous individuals, and it came off. But no less outstanding was the detailed forethought that went into the U.S. Navy crossing, which was backed by a well-planned route, a carefully organised system of radio communication and weather reports, air/sea rescue back-up, and nearly 100 ships spaced out along the route to support the flying-boats and their crews.

Specification of Navy-Curtiss NC 7A

Engines: Four 400 h.p. Liberty 12 Vee-type.
Span: 126 ft. 0 in. (38·40 m.).
Length: 68 ft. 3 in. (20·80 m.).
Wing area: 2,380·0 sq. ft. (221·11 sq. m.).
Take-off weight: 27,386 lb. (12,422 kg.).
Maximum speed: 91 m.p.h. (146 km/hr.) at sea level.
Service ceiling: 4,500 ft. (1,370 m.).
Normal range: 1,470 miles (2,366 km.).

---

18. Vickers Vimy

'I really do not know what we should admire most in our guests – their audacity, their determination, their skill, their science, their Vickers Vimy aeroplane, their Rolls-Royce engines, or their good fortune.' These were the words with which Winston Churchill, Secretary of State for War and Air, presented a cheque for £10,000 to Captain John Alcock and Lieutenant Arthur Whitten Brown at the Savoy Hotel, London, on 20 June 1919. Five days earlier, nose-down in an Irish bog, their aircraft had arrived at the end of one of the greatest flights in aviation history.

The £10,000 prize which they won had first been offered in 1913 by the *Daily Mail* newspaper, for the first direct (i.e. non-stop) aeroplane crossing to be made in under 72 hours between any point in the British Isles and one in Newfoundland, Canada or the United States. The Vimy, chosen by Alcock and Brown, was the 13th of these bombers off the Weybridge production line, stripped of its armament and bomb racks, and fitted with extra fuselage fuel tanks increasing the total capacity from 516 to 865 Imperial gallons (2,345 to 3,932 litres). Alcock took it up for the maiden test flight on 18 April 1919, and soon afterwards it was crated and shipped to Newfoundland, where it was reassembled at Quidi Vidi.

From Lester's Field, St John's, at 12½ minutes past four GMT, on the afternoon of 14 June 1919, the Vimy lurched into the air to begin its momentous journey. Soon it ran into the Newfoundland fog bank, the beginning of seven hours' unbroken fog before a brief respite of clear weather intervened; this was followed by stormy weather, iced-up instruments and control surfaces – and more fog. Once the aircraft lost considerable height, and was nearly into the sea before Alcock could right it; the airspeed indicator failed before the Vimy had covered half its journey; and Brown frequently had to clamber up above his seat to clear snow off the fuel flow indicators mounted on the centre-section struts (which, if they showed white, meant that fuel flow had stopped). Eventually, however, after flying 'blind' most of the way due to darkness and the weather, the first landfall was made: two small islands off the Galway Coast. After gaining the Irish mainland, Alcock circled the radio station at Clifden before landing in a nearby 'field' – in fact, the Derrygimla bog, into which the wheels sank, causing the Vimy to tip on to its nose. (The nose-landing wheel had been removed in Newfoundland, to save weight and drag.) The journey of 1,890 miles (3,041 km) had been made in a flying time of 16 hours 27½ minutes (15 hours 57 minutes coast-to-coast) at an average flying speed, aided by tail-winds, of 118 m.p.h. (190 km/hr.).

In addition to the *Daily Mail* prize, both Alcock and Brown received knighthoods from King George V. Alcock, sadly, was killed in December of the same year in a flying accident near Rouen, ironically while trying to land in fog. Knighthoods were also bestowed for another Vimy flight of 1919, this time upon the brothers Ross and Keith Smith, whose civil-registered G-EAOU (nicknamed 'God 'Elp All Of Us') made an equally hazardous and perhaps equally significant flight, in stages, from England (Hounslow) to Australia (Port Darwin) between 12 November and 10 December. Both Vimys, happily, are still in existence: the Alcock and Brown machine in the

---

Specification of Vickers Vimy

Engines: Two 360 h.p. Rolls-Royce Eagle VIII Vee-type.
Span: 69 ft. 7 in. (21·21 m.).
Length: 43 ft. 6½ in. (13·27 m.).
Wing area: 1,318·0 sq. ft. (122·44 sq. m.).
Take-off weight: 14,000 lb. (6,350 kg.).
Cruising speed: 90 m.p.h. (145 km/hr.).
Optimum range: 2,440 miles (3,927 km.).

Science Museum in London, and the Smiths' aircraft at Adelaide. It is a measure of Alcock and Brown's achievement that not for another eight years did another aeroplane (Lindbergh's) fly non-stop across the Atlantic – and that a full 20 years had to elapse before regular commercial services over this route began.

19. Junkers F 13

First flown on 25 June 1919, the little Junkers F 13 was one of the true pioneers of commercial air transport and ancestor of the metal transport aircraft that were to follow it during the 1920s and 1930s. Stemming from the wartime J 10 attack monoplane, it was a further practical application of the patent taken out in 1910 by Dr Hugo Junkers for thick-section monoplane wings of cantilever construction – wings which, in the F 13, were made up of no fewer than nine spars braced with welded duralumin tubes to give an immensely strong structure. The entire airframe, including control surfaces, was clad in corrugated duralumin sheet. The prototype was powered originally by a 160 h.p. Mercedes D.IIIa engine, but in early production aircraft a change was made to the 185 h.p.

B.M.W. IIIa, the unit which, as already described, made such a remarkable difference to the performance of the wartime Fokker D.VII.

The F 13 became widespread in service in almost every part of the world, the largest fleet being that of the manufacturer's own transport company, Junkers Luftverkehr, which between 1921 and 1926 had upwards of sixty F 13s in service. They flew some 15 million km (9·3 million miles), carrying nearly 282,000 passengers, before being absorbed into the D.L.H. fleet in 1926. Five years later, D.L.H. still had forty-three F 13s, exactly half of the total then in service with eight European airlines. The oft-quoted F 13 production total of 332 – in 60–70 different variants – is now thought to be an underestimate, a view apparently supported by the present-day MBB, which incorporates the former Junkers company and which recently quoted a round figure of 350. The first commercial aeroplane to be fitted with seat belts, the F 13 carried a crew of two and four passengers in the fully-enclosed cabin.

Complete examples of the F 13 are now rare indeed, but specimens are to be found in the collections of the Musée de l'Air in Paris, the Technical Museum in Stockholm, and the Kozlekedesi Museum in Budapest.

Specification of Junkers F 13a

Engine: One 185 h.p. B.M.W. IIIa in-line.
Span: 58 ft. 2¾ in. (17·75 m.).
Length (ex cluding skis): 31 ft. 6 in. (9·60 m.).
Wing area: 473·6 sq. ft. (44·00 sq. m.).
Take-off weight: 3,814 lb. (1,730 kg.).
Cruising speed: 87 m.p.h. (140 km/hr.).
Service ceiling: approx. 13,125 ft. (4,000 m.).
Endurance: 5 hr. 0 min.

---

20. Dornier Wal

By the time of its first flight on 6 November 1922, Dornier had already made arrangements for the Wal flying-boat to be built in Italy, to circumvent its inability to manufacture aircraft in Germany because of the terms of the Armistice Agreement. Eventually, some 300 Wals were to be built, not only in Italy but in Japan, the Netherlands, Spain, Switzerland and the U.S.A.; and eventually, the Wal was built in Germany as well. Probably the most famous Wals were those flown by Kapitän Wolfgang von Gronau of Germany and Commandante Rámon Franco of Spain. Von Gronau, with D-1422 *Amundsen Wal,* one of two early-production open-cockpit Wals used by Roald Amundsen in 1925 for Arctic survey and an attempt to reach the North Pole, made his first Atlantic crossing between 20–26 August 1930, from the island of Sylt via Iceland, Greenland and Halifax to New York – the first east–west crossing to be made by a flying-boat. In the following year, the newer D-2053 *Grönland Wal* carried him on a similar flight that extended as far as Chicago; and, in 1932, on a world flight that continued beyond Chicago to Milwaukee, the Rockies, Alaska, Japan, the Dutch East Indies, India, Arabia, Greece, Italy, and finally back to Sylt.

Well before von Gronau's exposition of the Wal's abilities, however, a Spanish crew had taken one of the very first Wals on an equally notable flight across the South Atlantic. Spain had been the first customer for the Wal, initially buying six, and on 22 January 1926 the fifth of these (M-MWAL *Plus Ultra,* almost identical to the Wal illustrated, but with 450 h.p. Napier Lions instead of the standard 300 h.p. Hispano-Suiza engines) left Palos de Moguer, the port from which Columbus had sailed for America. With Franco on board were Captain Julio Ruiz de Alda (navigator), Lt Juan Durán, engineer Pablo Rado, and a photographer, Leopoldo Alonso. Flying via Las Palmas, Porto Praia, Fernando de Noronha, Pernambuco, Rio de Janeiro and Montevideo, they arrived in Buenos Aires on 10 February 1926, after a 6,258 mile (10,072 km) journey completed in 59½ hours' flying. King Alfonso XIII of Spain subsequently donated *Plus Ultra* to the Argentine government, and it is today in the possession of the Lujan Museum in Argentina – the only surviving Wal in the world, so far as is known.

**Specification of
Dornier Wal**

Engines: Two 300 h.p. Hispano-Suiza Vee-type.
Span: 73 ft. 9¾ in. (22·50 m.).
Length: 58 ft. 2¾ in. (17·25 m.).
Wing area: 1,033·3 sq. ft. (96·00 sq. m.).
Take-off weight: 12,566 lb. (5,700 kg.).
Maximum cruising speed: 96 m.p.h. (155 km/hr.).
Service ceiling: 11,480 ft. (3,500 m.).
Range: approx. 1,245 miles (2,000 km.).

---

21. Douglas World Cruiser

If the pre-planning and preparation for the NC-4's transatlantic flight was impressive, that which preceded the round-the-world flight attempt by the U.S. Army Air Service's Douglas World Cruisers was nothing short of prodigious. Apart from the need to obtain permission for landings or overflights from no fewer than twenty-eight countries, involving fifteen different governments – a daunting exercise in diplomacy in itself – there was the Herculean task of organising fuel supplies, servicing and maintenance facilities, accommodation and the hundred and one other facilities that might be required en route.

Taking up the notion of a world flight in the spring of 1923, the U.S.A.A.S. obtained official War Department approval in the following December. By that time, on 10 October 1923, the prototype had already flown of the aircraft chosen for the flight: the World Cruiser, a specially adapted version of Douglas's DT-2 torpedo bomber with alternative wheel or float landing gear. The planned route was divided into six divisions, each in charge of an Advance Officer to smooth the aircraft's progress through his particular region.

The four appointed DWCs left Clover Field, California, on 17 March 1924 for Seattle, their starting-point, where they were fitted with floats and named *Seattle* (1), *Chicago* (2), *Boston* (3) and *New Orleans* (4). They were crewed, respectively, by Major Frederick L. Martin and Sgt A. L. Harvey; 1st Lts Lowell H. Smith and L. P. Arnold; 1st Lt L. Wade and Sgt H. H. Ogden; and 1st Lt Erik H. Nelson and 2nd Lt J. Harding. Martin was overall commander of the flight, and Nelson, to whom belongs much of the credit for its successful execution, was equipment and engineering officer. At 08·47 hours on 6 April the four floatplanes left Lake Washington, Seattle, on the first leg. *Seattle* was an early casualty, Martin flying into the side of a mountain in blinding snow on 30 April during the Chignik–Dutch Harbor leg, but the other three flew on across Arctic and tropic oceans, across glaciers, forests, deserts and jungles until, on 3 August, an oil pressure failure forced *Boston* down on to the water at Hornafiord, where it was subsequently wrecked during a salvage attempt on it. The DWC prototype, christened *Boston II*, flew out from America to join *Chicago* and *New Orleans* at Picton, whence all three completed the remainder of the homeward journey safely, landing back at Seattle at 13.30 hours on 28 September 1924.

To chronicle the log of the World Cruisers fully would require an entire book, but a full itinerary of their route, with stage lengths and flying times, is given in Appendix 1. Statistics for such a flight, such as the wearing out of twenty engines or the consumption of 68,950 U.S. gallons (260,943 litres) of fuel and 8,738 U.S. gallons (33,076 litres) of oil, are almost meaningless. Better, perhaps, to visualise what it meant in flying terms by realising that the only basic flying instruments were airspeed indicator, turn-and-bank indicator and altimeter; that no radio equipment was carried; and that the DWC's ceiling of 11,000 ft. (3,350 m.) – only 7,000 ft. (2,135 m.) in its seaplane form – did not allow it to climb above much of the weather which it met en route. Neither were there parachutes or lifejackets, though other survival equipment in each aircraft included a rifle, two pistols, fishing-tackle, vacuum-flasks of concentrated food, a first-aid kit, engine spares and tools – and a 60 lb. (27 kg.) ship's anchor and 150 ft. (46 m.) of tow rope. A final word on the reliability of the Liberty engines: despite the number used up, their average mileage flown, including a triumphal tour of the U.S. after their return, was 4,794 miles (7,715 km). *Chicago* can be found today in the National Air and Space Museum in Washington, and *New Orleans* in the U.S. Air Force Museum at Dayton, Ohio.

**Specification of
Douglas World Cruiser**
Engine: One 420 h.p. Liberty 12 Vee-type. Following data are for seaplane version:
Span: 50 ft. 0 in. (15·24 m.).
Length: approx. 39 ft. 4 in. (11·99 m.).
Wing area: 724·0 sq. ft. (67·26 sq. m.).
Maximum take-off weight: 8,180 lb. (3,710 kg.).
Cruising speed: approx. 85 m.p.h. (137 km/hr.).
Service ceiling: 7,000 ft. (2,135 m.).
Range: 1,650 miles (2,655 km.).

---

22. de Havilland Moth

Geoffrey de Havilland could scarcely have chosen a more apt or evocative name for the little D.H.60 two-seat biplane with which he took the world of light aviation by storm. Combining the epitome of de Havilland's design artistry with Major Frank Halford's 60 h.p. ADC Cirrus engine – evolved from half a Renault V-8 – the prototype which first flew on 22 February 1925 was to give rise to a whole family of brothers, sisters and cousins which stayed in production for twenty-two years.

The Moth's immediate impact was upon the British flying club movement, for which they were painted yellow (London), green (Midlands), blue (Lancashire) or red (Newcastle), with silver wings; in its later career it was private runabout, racer, record-breaker, air taxi, aerobatic champion. Following the original Cirrus or Genet version, as the years went by, came the DH60G Gipsy Moth, DH60M 'Metal Moth', DH60GIII Moth Major, DH75 Hawk Moth, DH80 Puss Moth (monoplane), DH82 Tiger Moth, DH83 Fox Moth, DH85 Leopard Moth (monoplane), DH 87 Hornet Moth, and the DH94 Moth Minor – not to mention a few incidental ones in between. They totalled more than 11,700 aircraft, of which about 8,750 were World War 2 Tiger Moth trainers, many of them built in

Australia, New Zealand and Canada. Of the others, none quite matched in popularity the original Cirrus/Genet Moth, of which more than 450 were built, or its immediate successor the DH60G or M (over 1,160) – though the Puss Moth (over 280 built) was nearly as popular as the original model.

It was in a Puss Moth (G-ABXY *The Heart's Content*) that James A. Mollison became, in 1932–33, the first man to fly solo east to west across both the North and South Atlantic, and the first to fly from England to South America. It was well said, in a recent reference to the Moth, that it would be hard to find any great British aviator whose logbook did not record some time spent in a Moth of one kind or another, and a list of names from Moth lore that includes Lady Bailey, C. A. Nepean Bishop, Hubert Broad, H. F. Broadbent, Alan Cobham, John Grierson, Alex Henshaw, Bert Hinkler, C. W. A. Scott and many, many others, leaves such a remark in no dispute whatever.

But if one must single out one name to epitomise the personal combination of pilot and aeroplane, few would dispute the right to that position of the twenty-seven-year-old Amy Johnson who, with less than 100 hours of solo flying behind her, set out from Croydon at 7.30 a.m. on 5 May 1930 in her faithful *Jason* to fly to Australia. Nineteen and a half days later, on 24 May, when she touched down at Darwin, she had not broken Hinkler's 15½ day record time, and she was not the first pilot – though she was the first woman pilot – to fly from England to Australia. But for sheer personal courage and sheer aeroplane reliability her flight in *Jason* – now hanging proudly in the Science Museum's Aeronautical Gallery in London – must take some beating. Possibly as many as 500 Moths of one kind or another can still be found in the world today, most

---

**Specification of
de Havilland Gipsy Moth**

Engine: One 100 h.p. de Havilland Gipsy I in-line.
Span: 30 ft. 0 in. (9·14 m.).
Length: 23 ft. 11 in. (7·29 m.).
Wing area: 243·0 sq. ft. (22·58 sq. m.).
Take-off weight: 1,650 lb. (748 kg.).
Cruising speed: 83 m.p.h. (134 km/hr.).
Service ceiling: 18,000 ft. (5,486 m.).
Range: 1,000 miles (1,610 km.).

of them Tiger Moths, which are still a favourite of private and professional pilots. Probably the oldest survivor is G-EBLV, the eighth production Moth, happily still airworthy with the Shuttleworth Collection, and, equally happily, incorporating within its airframe some parts from G-EBKT, the original Moth prototype.

23. Fokker tri-motor

The story of the Fokker tri-motor in commercial service can be found in *Airliners Between the Wars*, but in aviation history it is also linked indissolubly with two historic events: the first flight by an aeroplane over the North Pole, and the first aerial crossing of the Pacific Ocean by that great Australian aviator Charles Kingsford Smith. The polar aircraft, flown for the first time on 4 September 1925, was named *Josephine Ford* and made its 1,600 mile (2,575 km) flight over the North Pole in just under 16 hours on 9 May 1926, with Floyd Bennett as pilot and Lt Cdr Richard E. Byrd as navigator. Bennett later piloted another Fokker tri-motor, *America*, on a transatlantic flight to Paris in July 1927, only a few weeks

after Lindbergh's epic flight in the *Spirit of St. Louis*; and any list of famous Fokker flights must also include that by the float-equipped NX4204 *Friendship* on 17–18 June 1928, in which Amelia Earhart became the first woman to fly an aeroplane across the North Atlantic. But probably the best-known Fokker of them all was 'Smithy's' *Southern Cross*, which began life as *Detroiter*, bought by the famous explorer Sir Hubert Wilkins for use on the 1926 Arctic expedition sponsored by the *Detroit News*.

A hybrid aircraft, with the fuselage of an F.VIIa and the wings of an F.X, it was reconditioned by Boeing (and fitted with a quite un-Fokker-like rudder) before being sold to Kingsford Smith, minus engines, for £3,000. Fitted with three Wright Whirlwind J-5C engines, it was first used for a fifty-hour flight that just was not quite long enough to beat the existing endurance record. This flight, however, stood it in good stead for its next major achievement: a 7,389 mile (11,890 km) three-stage flight across the Pacific between 31 May and 9 June 1928, from Oakland Field, San Francisco, via Honolulu and Suva (Fiji) to Eagle Farm Airfield, Brisbane. Pilot on the flight was C. T. P. Ulm, and the third and fourth crew members were Harry Lyon (navigator) and James Warner (radio operator).

Later that year, on 10–11 September, with Ulm and a different crew, *Southern Cross* and Kingsford Smith made the first aerial crossing of the Tasman Sea between Australia (Sydney) and New Zealand (Christchurch) in 14½ hours. On 24–25 May 1930, *Southern Cross* made, in 31½ hours, the second east–west crossing of the North Atlantic (Portmarnock to Harbour Grace, Newfoundland), then completing its circumnavigation of the globe by flying across the U.S. continent back to San Francisco. In 1932 Kingsford Smith was knighted for his services to aviation, and in July

1935 made his last flight in *Southern Cross*. It was acquired by the National Museum in Canberra in 1941, restored to flying condition in 1945, made its last flight in 1946, and in 1958 went on special permanent display in its own hall at Eagle Farm Airport, Brisbane. The *Josephine Ford* also survives, as an exhibit in the Henry Ford Museum at Dearborn, Michigan.

24. Ford tri-motor

It takes a little stretching of the imagination to picture this five-ton, three-engined all-metal machine being thrown about the sky in loops, snap rolls and similar aerobatic manoeuvres, though we are assured that this has been done. On the other hand, no such elasticity is required to believe that the company responsible for America's Ford Reliability Tour should have produced one of the most dependable aeroplanes ever to have flown.

A faithful servant of commercial and privately-owned air transport services for many a long year, the fifty-year-old 'Tin Goose' (it first flew on 11 June 1926) even now has not entirely disappeared from sight; indeed, it was not so many years ago that

Specification of Fokker F. VII b-3m
Engines: Three 237 h.p. Wright J-5C Whirlwind radials.
Span: 71 ft. 2¼ in. (21·69 m.).
Length: 47 ft. 7 in. (14·50 m.).
Wing area: 728·0 sq. ft. (67·63 sq. m.).
Take-off weight: 15,348 lb. (6,962 kg.).
Cruising speed: 106 m.p.h. (170 km/hr.).

another American company attempted to market a reincarnated version, with modern engines, known as the Bushmaster 2000. That there was more to the Ford tri-motor than the shape of a Fokker and the skin of a Junkers was clearly apparent to Lt Cdr (later Rear-Admiral) Richard E. Byrd, U.S.N., the famous polar explorer. In 1926 Byrd had taken part in the first flight over the North Pole, and he was keen to achieve a 'double' by doing likewise over the South Pole.

As though bent on confusing future historians, he had named the Arctic Fokker after a member of the Ford family; for the Antarctic Expedition, he chose a Ford aeroplane and named it after the pilot of the Fokker, Floyd Bennett. Sadly, he was not to have Bennett, who had died of pneumonia, as his pilot in Antarctica, but he was fortunate in having instead the Norwegian Bernt Balchen, one of the greatest names in polar aviation – and, for that matter, in many other branches of aviation.

A two-year polar expedition had to be organised before the South Polar flight could be attempted, but at last, on 28 November 1929, the *Floyd Bennett* took off from its base at Little America, carrying Balchen and Byrd (pilot and navigator), Harold I. June (radio operator) and Capt. A. C. McKinley (surveyor). It reached the South Pole slightly less than 10 hours later, after vital food had been jettisoned in order to reduce weight and enable the Ford to climb above the Queen Maud mountains. Over the Pole, Byrd dropped an American flag, weighted with a stone from Floyd Bennett's grave. Nineteen hours after take-off, the reliable Ford tri-motor landed back at Little America, following a completely uneventful return trip, to leave Byrd with the distinction of being the first to reach both Poles by air. The *Floyd Bennett* still survives in the Henry Ford Museum at Dearborn, Michigan.

**Specification of
Ford Model 4-AT**

Engines: Three 300 h.p. Wright Whirlwind radials.
Span: 74 ft. 0 in. (22·56 m.).
Length: 49 ft. 10 in. (15·19 m.).
Wing area: 785·0 sq. ft. (72·93 sq. m.).
Take-off weight: 15,000 lb. (6,804 kg.).
Cruising speed: 107 m.p.h. (172 km/hr.).
Service ceiling: 16,500 ft. (5,030 m.).
Range: 1,140 miles (1,835 km.).

It is perhaps worth adding, as a postscript, that not for another twenty-seven years did an aeroplane actually land at the South Pole; this was the Douglas R4D-5 *Que Sera Sera*, which forms the subject of colour plate 33.

25. Ryan NYP

'CAN YOU CONSTRUCT WHIRL-WIND ENGINE PLANE CAPABLE FLYING NONSTOP BETWEEN NEW YORK AND PARIS STOP IF SO PLEASE STATE COST AND DELI-VERY DATE.' So ran the telegram that arrived on T. Claude Ryan's desk on 3 February 1927. Ryan thought he could, and told the enquirer, Robertson Aircraft Corporation of St Louis, that he could complete such an aeroplane in two months at a cost of $6,000, less engine and instruments. Robertson were the backers of a twenty-five-year-old air-mail pilot, Charles A. Lindbergh, and the objective was the $25,000 prize offered in 1919 by hotelier Raymond Orteig for the first non-stop flight between New York and Paris.

After seven years the prize had still not been won, though it had already claimed the life, in a take-off accident, of France's World War I ace of aces, René Fonck. In early 1927, two other contenders were preparing to bid for the prize: Lt Cdr Richard Byrd and a crew of three in the Fokker tri-motor *America*, and Clarence Chamberlin in the single-engined Bellanca W.B.2 *Columbia*; hence the urgency of Robertson's telegram. Lindbergh, who had never flown further than 500 miles (805 km) in his life before, was then little known, and his chances were not rated highly. Not, that is, until he arrived at New York on 12 May after a one-stop coast-to-coast flight from San Diego that clearly demonstrated the capability of both pilot and aeroplane.

Eight days later, at 07.52 hours on 20 May, the *Spirit of St Louis* took off from Roosevelt Field on Long Island with 450 U.S. gallons (1,703 litres) of fuel, and Lindbergh set course for Newfoundland on his Great Circle route to Paris. Some two-thirds of this fuel was in the fuselage, immediately behind the engine, with Lindbergh seated in a cramped and starkly simple cockpit behind the huge main tank. He had no forward view, except through a periscope to his left, and only the essential mini-mum of instruments. For much of the way he flew in rain, fog or darkness, mostly at low altitude;

and at 22.24 hours on 21 May he touched down at Paris (Le Bourget) airfield, to be mobbed by a huge and near-hysterical crowd. 'Speaking was impossible,' he wrote later. 'No words could be heard in the uproar and nobody apparently wanted to hear any. I started to climb out of the cockpit, but as soon as one foot appeared through the door I was dragged the rest of the way without any assistance on my part. For nearly half an hour I was unable to touch the ground, during which I was ardently carried around in what seemed to be a very small space, and in every position it is possible to be in.'

Statistically, he had flown 3,610 miles (5,809 km) in 33 hours 39 minutes at an average speed of 107·5 m.p.h. (173 km/hr.). But, more than that, Lindbergh's flight had fired the imagination of the world; he was fêted in France, Belgium and England, where he received the Légion d'Honneur and the Air Force Cross, before returning to America in the cruiser *Memphis* to a full-scale New York ticker-tape welcome. His little NYP (New York–Paris) monoplane now has an honoured place in the National Air and Space Museum in Washington, D.C. Of his rivals,

the *Columbia* – which Lindbergh had originally wanted to buy for his own attempt – was flown by Chamberlin and C. A. Levine from New York to Eisleben, Germany, on 4–6 June 1927, a flight some 300 miles (483 km) further than Lindbergh's. The Fokker *America* did not quite make Paris, having to come down off the French coast between Cherbourg and Le Havre on 30 June 1927.

**Specification of
Ryan NYP**

Engine: One 237 h.p. Wright J-5C Whirlwind radial.
Span: 46 ft. 0 in. (14·02 m.).
Length: 27 ft. 8 in. (8·43 m.).
Wing area: 319·0 sq. ft. (29·64 sq. m.).
Take-off weight: 5,250 lb. (2,381 kg.).
Maximum speed: 119·5 m.p.h. (192 km/hr.).
Range: 4,210 miles (6,775 km.).

---

26. Lockheed Vega

The Vega, probably the most famous of all of Lockheed's 'plywood bullets', first achieved fame when it swept the board in the National Air Race of 1930 by taking all of the first five places for the 1,760 mile (2,832 km) non-stop event. In later years it became associated with many of the great names in U.S. aviation history – Jimmy Doolittle, Amelia Earhart, James J. Mattern and Roscoe Turner, to name only four – but with none more closely than that of Wiley Post, the one-eyed airman who was personal pilot to oilman F. C. Hall of Oklahoma City. Post's black eye-patch was an instant recognition feature, and an appropriate one, for it was with the insurance money from the accident that cost him his left eye that he paid for his first flying lessons. In August 1930 he won the National, from Los Angeles to Chicago, in just over 9 hours 9 minutes, in the second of two Vegas to be owned by Hall and named *Winnie Mae* after his (Hall's) daughter.

Within less than a year, this domestic success was to be overshadowed by international achievement, when Post recaptured from Germany's airship *Graf Zeppelin* the record for a flight around the world. Taking Tasmanian-born Harold Gatty, a Los Angeles navigation instructor, as his only crewman, Post took off in the Vega 5B *Winnie Mae* from Roosevelt Field, Long Island, at 05.00 hours on the morning of 23 June 1931, and arrived back in the late evening of 1 July – a total elapsed time of 8 days 15 hours 51 minutes. Two years later this achievement was capped by a second world flight, between 15–22 July 1933, in which Post not only flew solo but cut some 21 hours off his previous record, and was afterwards presented by Hall with the aircraft. *Winnie Mae* then turned her talents in other directions.

In 1934, Post was engaged by the Goodrich company to help develop a pressure suit for altitudes above 50,000 ft. (15,240 m.), and in the course of these experiments decided to make an attempt at the world height record, then standing to an Italian aircraft at 47,352 ft. (14,433 m.). On the first attempt, the supercharger failed at 42,000 ft. (12,800 m.); on the second, *Winnie Mae* reached 51,000 ft. (15,545 m.); and on the third, 55,000 ft. (16,765 m.), this one being an unofficial barograph reading as the altimeter had frozen up. *Winnie Mae* was then fitted with a jettisonable undercarriage and a belly landing skid, and three further attempts were made. These altitude flights did much to evaluate flying conditions at such heights and prepare the way for the first pressure-cabin aircraft of the middle and late 1930s.

In early 1935, Post attempted to lower the trans-U.S. speed record in the *Winnie Mae*, but had to abandon the flight due to an overheating engine. He sold her in February of that year for a new Lockheed, a hybrid Orion/Explorer named *Blue Flash*, in which he set out in early August with film actor Will Rogers on a non-record, leisurely round-the-world flight in the opposite direction to his two earlier triumphs. This aeroplane crashed while taking off from an Alaskan

---

Specification of
Winnie Mae

Engine: One 450 h.p. Pratt & Whitney Wasp SC1 radial.
Span: 41 ft. 0 in. (12·49 m.).
Length: 27 ft. 6 in. (8·38 m.).
Wing area: 275·0 sq. ft. (25·55 sq. m.).
Take-off weight: 4,265 lb. (1,935 kg.).
Maximum speed: 180 m.p.h. (290 km/hr.).
Service ceiling: 24,000 ft. (7,315 m.).
Range: 1,000 miles (1,610 km.).

---

airstrip, and both occupants were killed. After Wiley Post's death, *Winnie Mae* was acquired by the Smithsonian Institution, whose halls she shares today with another famous Vega, that in which Amelia Earhart became the first woman to make a solo flight across the Atlantic.

27. Hawker Hart

It is the goal of every bomber designer to design a bomber that will be immune from attack by fighters, and in the context of the 1920s that meant one of two things – superior height or speed. Specification 12/26, issued by the Air Ministry, was so demanding in performance terms that many British manufacturers believed it impossible to meet. Two men who did not were Fred Sigrist and chief designer Sydney Camm of Hawkers, and at the Olympia Aero Exhibition of 1929 appeared what proved to be the archetypal Hawker biplanes of the next decade – the single-seat Hornet fighter, later to become the Fury, and the two-seat Hart day bomber. The Hart not only met but surpassed the demands of 12/26, its top speed of 184 m.p.h. (296 km/hr.) being a clear 10 m.p.h. (16 km/hr.) better than the R.A.F.'s current fighter, the Bristol Bulldog – which posed the R.A.F. not a few tactical problems and undoubtedly spurred its interest in the 200-

m.p.h.-plus (over 320 km/hr.) Fury.

During the late 1920s and early 1930s the Hart spawned a whole family of sister designs: Demon, Osprey, Audax, Hart Trainer, Hardy, Hector; and by 1934 seven out of every eight aircraft being delivered to the R.A.F. were of Hawker design. In all, more than 2,800 Hart variants were built, incidentally providing employment for many of the firms that had fought shy of the original specification, for production was sub-contracted to Armstrong Whitworth (456), Avro (244), Boulton Paul (106), Bristol (141), Gloster (144), Vickers (226) and Westland (43).

Two factors contributed to its success: its Rolls-Royce Kestrel engine, and its system of construction. The former offered a lightweight installation for the power available, and an excellent low-drag streamlined profile. The latter, for which credit must go chiefly to Sigrist, also combined strength with lightness, making extensive use of tubular steel main members with duralumin tube or flat-plate supporting structures, the whole ensemble being bolted or riveted, rather than welded, to simplify construction. Camm's design genius scarcely needs elabora-

tion: take away the top wing and fixed wheels of the Hart or Fury, and you have – more or less – the Hurricane of ten years later.

Specification of Hawker Hart
Engine: One 525 h.p. Rolls-Royce Kestrel IB Vee-type.
Span: 37 ft. 3 in. (11·35 m.).
Length: 29 ft. 4 in. (8·94 m.).
Wing area: 348·0 sq. ft. (32·33 sq. m.).
Take-off weight: 4,554 lb. (2,066 kg.).
Maximum speed: 184 m.p.h. (296 km/hr.) at 5,000 ft. (1,525 m.).
Service ceiling: 21,350 ft. (6,510 m.).
Range: 470 miles (756 km.).

28. Handley Page H.P.42

Sharing the July 1929 Aero Exhibition at Olympia, London, with Hawker's famous twosome were a scale model and a full-size passenger cabin mock-up of another aeroplane destined to have a long-term impact upon British aviation in the 1930s: the Handley Page H.P.42. Seldom can such a reputation have been earned by an aircraft of which so few were built, for at that time only a prototype had been ordered. Three more, at a cost of £21,000 each, were ordered before the year's end, and an option on a further five was taken up later. Yet these eight machines, the first of which entered service in 1931, proved so popular and so utterly reliable that they soldiered on long past their intended retirement in 1935, and all but one of them survived into the World War 2 period.

Typical examples of Handley Page's 'build 'em big' outlook, their design was the work of H. D. Boultbee, who described it as 'quite a quick job because I believe that if the basic idea is correct it goes down on paper as fast as one can draw'. He completed his tender drawings for Imperial Airways in six weeks; the prototype contract was placed on 15 April 1929, and the first flight was made on 14 November 1930. This aircraft, G-AAGX, was later named *Hannibal*, and was one of four 'Eastern' type H.P.42s (the others being *Hadrian*, *Hanno* and *Horsa*) designed to carry eighteen or twenty-four passengers and mail. The four 'Western' aircraft (*Heracles*, *Horatius*, *Hengist* and *Helena*) were designed for the airline's European services, carrying thirty-eight passengers and a smaller amount of mail.

Despite their archaic appearance, they had four great attractions, to operator and passengers alike: four-engined reliability, sturdy construction, first-class furnishing and catering, and effective cabin soundproofing. Between them they flew more than 10 million miles (16·09 million km), none of them flew less than 12,000 hours, and none of them ever killed a passenger. The only pre-war loss was *Hengist*, burned out in a hangar fire at Karachi in 1937 after conversion to Eastern configuration. Crashes destroyed *Horatius* in 1939, and *Hannibal* and *Horsa* in 1940, *Hannibal* disappearing during a flight over the Gulf of Oman. *Hadrian*, *Hanno* and *Heracles* were all wrecked on the ground by gales during 1940; and *Helena*, the last to go, was

---

Specification of Handley Page H.P.42

Engines: Four 555 h.p. Bristol Jupiter XFBM radials.
Span: 130 ft. 0 in. (39·62 m.).
Length: 89 ft. 9 in. (27·36 m.).
Wing area: 2,989·0 sq. ft. (277·69 sq. m.).
Maximum take-off weight: 28,000 lb. (12,700 kg.).
Maximum cruising speed: 105 m.p.h. (169 km/hr.).
Range: 250 miles (402 km.).

dismantled in August 1941. A propeller from *Heracles* survives in the Science Museum, London, and in 1975 another, from *Horatius*, was donated to the Exeter Flying Club.

29. Junkers Ju 52/3m

Sometimes described as Germany's counterpart of the Ford 'Tin Goose', the Junkers Ju 52/3m went by many other names during her long life: Pava (turkey) to the Nationalists in the Spanish Civil War, 'Iron Annie' or 'Corrugated Coffin' to the Allies in World War 2, and Toucan to the French in the early post-war years; but most often, and most affectionately, as 'Tante Ju' to her Luftwaffe crews and the Parachute and Wehrmacht troops who flew in her. Winner of no prizes for aesthetic appeal, she was roomy, noisy, draughty, docile, rugged and, above all, reliable. The sound of her three engines, of whatever type (and she had many) has been variously likened to a collection of unsynchronised lawn-mowers or half a dozen motor-cycles racing downhill in bottom gear. Yet she was easy (if laborious) to handle, and demanded a field length of only some 750 m. (2,460 ft.) from which to operate with full load.

A tri-motor development by Dipl.-Ing. Ernst Zendel of the single-engined Ju 52 of 1930, the Ju 52/3m first flew in April 1931 and remained in steady production in Germany from 1932 to 1944; including foreign manufacture, the total built was close on 5,000, and Hitler chose one of the early production aircraft (D-2600 *Immelmann*) as his personal transport. First commercial services, by D.L.H., began in June 1932, and two years later the first bomber-transports were delivered to the still-clandestine Luftwaffe.

Career as a bomber was short-lived, but in the transport role the Ju 52/3m became one of the most adaptable and best-known types ever built. Nearly 200 entered service with some thirty airlines before World War 2, and during the war the Luftwaffe made prolific and prodigal use of the 'Tante Ju' as troop and Fallschirmjäger transport and supply aircraft, ambulance, glider tug, mine clearer and for many other tasks. More than 570 took part in the invasion of Norway and Denmark in April 1940, and almost as many in France and the Low Countries a month later. In due course the Ju 52/3m appeared in the campaigns in Greece, North Africa, Crete and Russia, and is credited by some with playing a larger part in shaping the course of the air war than any Axis combat aircraft. It was the last of a long line of Junkers corrugated aircraft, and a few examples can still be found in service in the mid-1970s, after an operational lifetime of almost forty years.

**Specification of
Junkers Ju 52/3m**

Engines: Three 600 h.p.
B.M.W. 132A-3 radials.
Span: 95 ft. 11½ in. (29·25 m.).
Length: 62 ft. 0 in. (18·90 m.).
Wing area: 1,189·4 sq. ft.
(110·50 sq. m.).
Take-off weight: 20,944 lb.
(9,500 kg.).
Maximum speed: 172 m.p.h.
(277 km/hr.) at 3,280 ft.
(1,000 m.).
Service ceiling: 19,360 ft.
(5,900 m.).
Range: 620 miles (1,000 km.).

---

30. Taylor/Piper Cub

In May 1972 the Cessna Aircraft Company became the first aircraft manufacturer in the world to pass the milestone of 100,000

aeroplanes produced, a total achieved in forty-five years of operation. Another company now boasting that figure is Piper Aircraft Corporation, whose output of aircraft passed the 100,000 mark in 1976. The Piper figure is the more remarkable when it is remembered that about half of that total is made up of sales of a basic design which, apart from a natural process of refinement and a steady increase in available power, has changed very little since it first appeared in 1931. This aeroplane had its origins two years earlier, during the Depression, when an oil company executive decided to invest $400 in the Taylor Brothers Aircraft Corporation, a small private company then struggling to market a two-seat side-by-side lightplane known as the Chummy. They sold six. Two years later the company became the Taylor Aircraft Company Inc., and William T. Piper was appointed its secretary and treasurer.

Piper confessed to knowing nothing about aviation, but he had an instinct for the kind of lightplane that he felt people would buy, and inspired Taylor to design it. It was a tandem two-seater, simpler to build than a motor-car, and could be marketed for $1,325 – about a quarter the price of other two-seat light aircraft then on the market. They named it the Cub, and it made its first flight, powered by a 37 h.p. Continental flat-four engine, in February 1931. This first model, the Taylor E-2, was followed by the F-2 (1935) and the J-2 (1936) before Piper and Taylor parted, the former creating his own company in 1937.

Piper introduced the J-3 Cub in 1938, and after the outbreak of World War 2 mass production of the Cub as the L-4 Grasshopper for the U.S. armed forces really took off. By mid-1941 Piper was turning them out at a rate of 400 a month, and by 1949 total production of military and civil versions had reached nearly 20,000. This was the year in which the Cub gave way to the Super Cub, certificated in November with a 90 or 108 h.p. engine. The Super was still in production in 1976, now with a 150 h.p. flat-four, and matches its predecessor in overall numbers built. It has not, by any means, been roses all the way, but that $400 investment has now become a $30 million family fortune. There are Pipers galore still flying around the world today, and it is even possible to find a few examples of the earliest E-2 models still surviving.

Specification of Piper L-21B
Engine: One 135 h.p. Lycoming O-290-D2 flat-four.
Span: 35 ft. 3 in. (10·74 m.).
Length: 22 ft. 5 in. (6·83 m.).
Wing area: 178·5 sq. ft. (16·58 sq. m.).
Take-off weight: 1,500 lb. (680 kg.).
Maximum speed: 127 m.p.h. (204 km/hr.).
Service ceiling: 19,000 ft. (5,790 m.).
Maximum range: 500 miles (805 km.).

31. Boeing 247

An unkind historian might claim that the Boeing 247 was the aeroplane which gave the world the Douglas DC-3 – and in a sense he would be right. But this would hardly be a fair judgement of an aeroplane which itself was not only innovative but highly versatile as well. Born in the early 1930s as a replacement for the three-engined Model 80 biplanes of Boeing Air Transport, the 247 was based on design techniques and methods already proved in Boeing's B-9 twin-engined bomber and Monomail single-engined mailplane; it was twin-engined (for better performance and operating costs), and was an all-metal cantilever low-wing monoplane with a retractable landing gear – a complete opposite to the wood-and-fabric, fixed-gear biplanes and high-wing monoplanes then used by most of the world's major airlines.

Boeing designers wanted to make it bigger, but B.A.T. got its way in demanding a smaller aircraft, and the giant United Aircraft Transport Corporation, of which B.A.T. was a part, ordered a staggering total of sixty virtually 'off the drawing board'. (Another fifteen were built later.) As a result, U.A.T.C. tied up the production line at Seattle, and T.W.A., rendered unable to order 247s, went instead to Donald W. Douglas, who designed the DC-1 – larger and 35 m.p.h. (56 km/hr.) faster than the 247, and the forerunner of the DC-2 and DC-3. Result: the 247, which went into service with United in mid-1933, was outmoded within a year of beginning operations. The final blow came in November 1935, when United leased thirty of its Boeings to feeder companies and bought ten DC-3s.

None of this, however, can detract from the significance of what the 247 represented. It heralded the beginning of the era of clean, fast, modern air transport aircraft; it introduced many new features, such as supercharged engines and cabin air-conditioning, for the first time, and was the first airliner able to climb on one engine with a full load; it cut the coast-to-coast journey time across the U.S.A. from 28 hours to 16, in its definitive 247D form; and it gave excellent service into and after World War 2 not only as an airliner but as a military transport, executive and cargo transport, crop-sprayer, Arctic rescue or oil exploration aircraft and film star. In October 1944, in England, it added to this list by becoming the first aircraft in the world to make an automatic landing.

One of the best-remembered 247s, still preserved by the National Air and Space Museum in Washington, is that flown in the transport section of the 1934 'MacRobertson' air race from England to Australia by Col. Roscoe Turner and Clyde Pangbourn; a race in which, incidentally, it again took second place to the DC-2 . . .

**Specification of
Boeing 247D**

Engines: Two 550 h.p. Pratt
& Whitney Wasp S1H1-G
radials.
Span: 74 ft. 0 in. (22·56 m.).
Length: 51 ft. 7 in. (15·72 m.).
Wing area: 836·13 sq. ft.
(77·68 sq. m.).
Take-off weight: 13,650 lb.
(6,192 kg.).
Maximum cruising speed: 189
m.p.h. (304 km/hr.) at 12,000
ft. (3,660 m.).
Service ceiling: 25,400 ft.
(7,740 m.).
*Range at maximum cruising
speed:* 750 miles (1,207 km.).

32. Tupolev ANT-25

Design of the ANT-25 began in
1931 at the TsAGI (Central Aero
and Hydrodynamic Institute) in
Russia, where its alternative
designation RD (Rekord Dal-
nosti: Long-range Record) also
revealed its primary purpose. Its
more familiar designation revealed that the design team was
led by A. N. Tupolev – a team,
incidentally, that included another later-famous Soviet designer, Pavel Sukhoi. For its first
flight, by Col. Mikhail M. Gromov on 22 June 1933, it was
powered by an 874 h.p. M-34

engine, later uprated to 900 h.p.;
and it was this pilot, with A. I.
Filin and I. T. Spirin as crew,
who flew it on its first major long-
distance flight on 10–12 September the following year. This
was a flight from Moscow to
Ryazan via Tula, a distance of
7,712 miles (12,411 km) which it
covered in 75 hours 2 minutes at
an average speed of 95 m.p.h.
(153 km/hr.).

The Russians, however, had
their sights on a flight across the
North Pole to America, and this
was attempted on 3 August 1935
with a crew comprising S. A.
Levanevskii, G. F. Baidukov and
V. I. Levchenko; but they were
obliged to abandon the attempt
after covering some 3,730 miles
(6,000 km). In the following year,
on 20–22 July, an attempt was
made on the closed-circuit distance record by V. P. Chkalov,
Baidukov and A. V. Belya-
kov. The chosen route was
from Moscow via Franz Josef
Land, Severnaya Zemlya, Tiksi
and Petropavlovsk-Kamchatskii
back to Moscow, and with the
Soviet dictator's approval was
publicised as the Stalinskii Mar-
shrut (Stalin Route). This time
the ANT-25 covered some three-
quarters of the intended route –
a distance of 5,825 miles (9,374
km) – in 56 hours 20 minutes

flying time before having to make a landing near the Amur River in Siberia.

In November 1936 it attracted much attention at the Salon de l'Aéronautique in Paris, but its major efforts at a flight to the U.S.A. were still to come. On 18–20 June 1937 an aircraft registered NO 25, with a crew headed by Chkalov and an M-34R engine boosted to 950 h.p., reached the Washington township of Vancouver, near Seattle, a distance of 5,673 miles (9,130 km) from Moscow; but this was not a non-stop flight, having been broken in Alaska after covering 5,284 miles (8,504 km). A month later, however, a similar aircraft (NO 25–1), crewed by Gromov, Cmdt Andrei B. Yumashchev and Ing. Sergei A. Danilin, at last achieved the ANT-25's six-year-old objective. On 12–14 July these three airmen made a non-stop flight, from Moscow to San Jacinto, California, of 6,306 miles (10,148 km) in 62 hours 17 minutes at an average speed of 115 m.p.h. (185 km/hr.); and the record was theirs.

True to form, *Pravda* the following day felt obliged to sour a fine feat of airmanship by using its countrymen's achievement as the excuse for some typical sabre-rattling remarks; but most people, in Russia and elsewhere, will remember the ANT-25 for its intrinsic achievements, which apart from record attempts included a very real contribution towards the establishment of Arctic weather stations in Russia and the cause of polar aviation generally. One ANT-25 still survives, in the Chkalovsk Museum in the U.S.S.R.

**Specification of
Tupolev ANT-25**

Engine: One 950 h.p. M-34R Vee-type.
Span: 111 ft. 6½ in. (34·00 m.).
Length: 42 ft. 11 in. (13·08 m.).
Wing area: 949·4 sq. ft. (88·20 sq. m.).
Maximum take-off weight: 24,868 lb. (11,280 kg.).
Maximum speed: 153 m.p.h. (246 km/hr.).
Service ceiling: 9,850 ft. (3,000 m.).
Range: 8,080 miles (13,000 km.).

---

33. Douglas DC-1/2/3

In late 1975 and early 1976, as this book was being written, it was hardly possible to pick up any major aeronautical magazine without finding in it an article celebrating the 40th anniversary of the DC-3, which made its first flight on 17 December 1935 – itself the 32nd anniversary of the Wright brothers' first flight. As already mentioned, it was because U.A.T.C. made the Boeing 247 virtually its exclusive property that T.W.A. was obliged to shop elsewhere for a comparable transport, and the DC-1 which emerged as a result made its first flight on 1 July 1933, less than five months after the Boeing.

Its performance margin over the 247 was so much that it could afford to be made larger without surrendering its overall advantage, and so the initial production version was the DC-2, carrying fourteen passengers (compared with ten in the Boeing and twelve in the DC-1) and still cruising at about 40 m.p.h. (64 km/hr.) faster than the 247. T.W.A. eventually operated more than thirty DC-2s, beginning in August 1934, but the real triumph that year was that of K.L.M.'s DC-2 *Uiver*, which came first in its class (and second overall) in the great 'MacRobertson' race from England to Australia and really brought the Douglas Commercials into worldwide prominence.

And then, just as the need to compete with the Boeing 247 had sponsored the DC-1 and DC-2, so the need to compete with *them* gave rise to the DC-3, this time to meet the needs of American Airlines. In simple terms, the DC-3 was a DC-2 with a fuselage made wider, initially to provide 'sleeper' accommodation (still for fourteen passengers) and then, inevitably, to take an extra row of seats in place of the bunks and so carry twenty-one passengers. When offered a transport seating 50 per cent more than the DC-2, with only two-thirds the latter's operating costs, airlines fell over themselves to order DC-3s as fast as Douglas could build them, and by 1939 no less than *90 per cent* of the world's airline traffic was being flown by this one type. By the end of 1941, Douglas had built 455 DC-3s; by the end of World War 2 that total had passed the 10,000 mark, and its record as a war transport, as the C-47 Skytrain (and under a host of other designations and names, official and unofficial), is now legendary.

Some thousands poured back on to the commercial market after the war, a lot of them forming the basic equipment of many a new embryo airline, and others went to innumerable world air forces. Survivors today can still be counted in hundreds, and it is pleasant to record that, in mid-1975, one of the two surviving airworthy DC-2s was acquired by the Donald Douglas Museum in Santa Monica. During its career the DC-3 has done almost every flying job in the book (and probably more than a few that are not), and has unconcernedly survived innumerable attempts to replace it. It has earned itself a score of sobriquets, including Gooney Bird, Old Bucket-Seats, Spooky, 'Puff' the Magic Dragon and Grand Old Lady. But perhaps as appropriate as any on which to end is that of ZK-AOF, reluctantly sold in 1976 by New Zealand National Airways Corporation after a mere

---

Specification of Douglas R4D-5

Engines: Two 1,200 h.p. Pratt & Whitney R-1830-92 Twin Wasp radials.
Span: 95 ft. 0 in. (28·96 m.).
Length: 64 ft. 6 in. (19·66 m.).
Wing area: 987·0 sq. ft. (91·70 sq. m.).
Maximum take-off weight: 29,000 lb. (13,154 kg.).
Maximum cruising speed: 190 m.p.h. (306 km/hr.).
Service ceiling: 22,500 ft. (6,858 m.).
Maximum range: 2,150 miles (3,460 km.).

---

twenty-nine years of service. To N.Z.N.A.C., those registration letters stood for 'Allo Old Friend'; and it will, one feels, be a good many years yet before that 'allo' becomes 'farewell'.

34. Dornier Do 17

Spectators watching the International Military Aircraft Competition at Zurich in July 1937 were duly impressed, as well they might have been – and were no doubt meant to be – when the Circuit of the Alps event was won by a twin-engined German bomber that outstripped in performance every single-engined fighter racing against it. What they did not know, then, was that they were watching the eighth prototype of a design that had first flown nearly three years previously and was already entering service with the still-new Luftwaffe.

The Dornier Do 17 had originated as a six-passenger high-speed mailplane designed for Deutsche Luft Hansa, only to be rejected by the airline because it was so slim-bodied that it would have been difficult for passengers easily to gain access to their seats. These beautifully slender lines, which later gave rise to such nicknames as 'Eversharp' and 'Flying Pencil', were built for speed before comfort, and when by chance an ex-Dornier pilot, who was liaison officer between D.L.H. and the German Air Ministry, was able to fly one of the prototypes, he was soon able to generate interest in developing the Do 17 as a medium bomber.

One other point unknown to the Zürich spectators was that the top speed of 276 m.p.h. (444 km/hr.) shown by the V8 prototype was some 56 m.p.h. (90 km/hr.) better than that of the Do 17E then entering Luftwaffe service, thanks to various aerodynamic refinements and the use of 1,000 h.p. DB 600A engines instead of the 750 h.p. BMW VIs of the Do 17E. Even so, the Do 17 was still an advanced bomber for its time, and the E and F initial production models duly underwent an operational blooding in the Spanish Civil War during 1938–39.

They were superseded in service by the Do 17M and P series and finally by the Do 17Z. When production ended in 1940 about 1,100 Do 17s had been built, nearly half of these being Do 17Zs, the most numerous variant and the one most prominent in the Battle of Britain. The Do 17

line did not, however, end there, for it was developed progressively into the larger Do 215 and, from 1938, the Do 217 which became a mainstay of Luftwaffe bomber, night fighter and reconnaissance squadrons during the later years of the war.

Specification of Dornier Do 17E-1

Engines: Two 750 h.p. B.M.W.VI radials.
Span: 59 ft. 0⅔ in. (18·00 m.).
Length: 53 ft. 3¾ in. (16·25 m.).
Wing area: 592·0 sq. ft. (55·00 sq. m.).
Maximum take-off weight: 15,520 lb. (7,040 kg.).
Maximum speed: 220 m.p.h. (354 km/hr.) at sea level.
Service ceiling: 16,730 ft. (5,100 m.).
Operational radius: 311 miles (500 km.).

---

35. Polikarpov I-15

Nikolai Polikarpov was the doyen of Soviet fighter designers of the 1930s, and his best-known memorial is undoubtedly the I-15 series of single-seat biplanes. It was during this decade that the great military changeover from biplanes to monoplanes took place, but in 1932 the Soviet authorities decided to back both types of fighter, the former for their faster rate of climb and the latter for their better outright speed. Thus it was that Polikarpov embarked simultaneously upon two designs that were to become, respectively, the I-15 and I-16. They made their respective maiden flights in October and December 1933, the I-15 prototype being powered by a 700 h.p. M-25 engine. Armed with four forward-firing 7·62 mm. machine-guns and characterised by its gull-shaped upper wing, the I-15 was an excellent aircraft of its day and extremely manoeuvrable.

Further evidence of its performance came on 21 November 1935, when test pilot Vladimir Kokkinaki took a specially-lightened aircraft up to 47,818 ft. (14,575 m.) to set a new world altitude record. In the previous year work had already begun to evolve a new version – the I-15 bis or I-152 – which differed chiefly in having the upper wing raised on struts (to improve still further the pilot's field of view), a 750 h.p. M-25B engine in a long-chord N.A.C.A. cowling, and the ability to carry small bombs or drop-tanks beneath the lower wings.

Russia, the largest foreign contributor of aircraft to the forces engaged in the Spanish Civil War, sent more than 500 I-15 and I-15bis fighters to Spain, where they were promptly dubbed Chato (flat-nose); others were used in the Far East, notably in the Sino-Japanese 'Nomonhan Incident' of 1939. The third version – the I-15ter or I-153 – also served in Spain, earning the nickname Chaika (gull). This, evolved in 1935 by A. Y. Shcherbakov, reverted to the original upper-wing configuration (though of improved section), and had a more powerful engine and a retractable main landing gear. All three versions of the I-15 series served during the early years of World War 2, though by then obsolescent.

Specification of Polikarpov I-153

Engine: One 1,000 h.p. M-63 radial.
Span: 32 ft. 9¾ in. (10·00 m.).
Length: 20 ft. 3⅛ in. (6·175 m.).
Wing area: 238·3 sq. ft. (22·14 sq. m.).
Normal take-off weight: 4,189 lb. (1,900 kg.).
Maximum speed: 275 m.p.h. (443 km/hr.) at 9,850 ft. (3,000 m.).
Service ceiling: 36,000 ft. (11,000 m.).
Normal range: 298 miles (480 km.).

The I-153, with 1,000 h.p. engine, was one of the fastest biplane fighters ever to enter service, its nearest rivals for speed being the Gloster Gladiator and the Fiat C.R.42 – both of which had a fixed landing gear. The I-153 had, however, one little-known link with later Soviet fighter development: responsibility for its production was entrusted to a young designer named Artem Mikoyan. One I-153 still survives, in the Musée de l'Air in Paris.

36. Fairey Swordfish

The cancellation of Britain's TSR-2 'Canberra replacement' bomber in the mid-1960s is still recent enough history to be recalled by most readers; happily for Great Britain, such was not the fate forty years earlier of another similarly-designated British aircraft. This was the Fairey T.S.R. II, first flown on 17 April 1934 and later to become famous as the Swordfish torpedo-bomber and anti-submarine aircraft: a reliable, stable, tolerant and surprisingly manoeuvrable old lady, obsolescent at the outbreak of World War 2, yet in service from first to last, outliving her own intended replacement by two years and taking part in some of the war's most illustrious actions.

In September 1939 the Fleet Air Arm had thirteen Swordfish squadrons, a number which was to be doubled before the last front-line squadron was disbanded in May 1945. Their first wartime battle operations were off the Norwegian coast in the spring of 1940, and in November of that year they carried out the epic raid on the Italian fleet in Taranto harbour, crippling three battleships, one cruiser and two destroyers and sinking two auxiliaries for the loss of only two Swordfish.

Four months later, at Cape Matapan, they helped to disable another Italian cruiser; and then, in May 1941, came the dramatic encounter with the pocket battleship *Bismarck*. The first Swordfish attack was made on 24 May by No. 825 Squadron, led by Lt Cdr Eugene Esmonde, from H.M.S. *Victorious*, but made only one torpedo hit. *Bismarck* was then lost in the fog, but was re-sighted on 26 May, when she was attacked by Nos. 810 and 818 Squadrons from *Ark Royal*. In the second of these attacks her rudder was damaged by a torpedo strike, slowing her down sufficiently for her to be fired upon and sunk by the Royal Navy on the following day.

The Swordfish's last torpedo action, in February 1942, was as calamitous as it was gallant. Six aircraft of No. 825, again led by Esmonde, attacked in atrocious weather the warships *Scharnhorst*, *Gneisenau* and *Prinz Eugen* making their 'Channel Dash'. All six Swordfish, and thirteen of their eighteen crew members, were lost, including Esmonde, who was awarded posthumously the first Victoria Cross to go to a member of the Fleet Air Arm.

Thereafter the Swordfish,

equipped with A.S.V. (Air to Surface Vessel) radar and carrying depth charges or rocket projectiles, became a most effective submarine-hunter and a valuable protector of convoys in the Atlantic and Baltic – while its intended replacement, the Albacore, came off operations by the end of 1943. Known with universal affection as the 'Stringbag', the Swordfish was one of the great aeroplanes of its time. Today only a few survive, most of them in Britain and Canada, and of those only one is still airworthy.

**Specification of
Fairey Swordfish I**

Engine: One 690 h.p. Bristol Pegasus IIIM.3 radial.
Span: 45 ft. 6 in. (13·87 m.).
Length: landplane 36 ft. 4 in. (11·07 m.); floatplane 40 ft. 11 in. (12·47 m.).
Wing area: 607·0 sq. ft. (56·39 sq. m.).
Take-off weight (landplane): 9,250 lb. (4,196 kg.).
Maximum speed: 139 m.p.h. (224 km/hr.) at 4,750 ft. (1,450 m.).
Service ceiling: 10,700 ft. (3,260 m.).
Range with 1,610 lb. (730 kg.) torpedo: 546 miles (879 km.).

---

37. de Havilland D.H.88 Comet

Rightly regarded as the first 'trans-world' air race, and still remembered as one of the greatest, the 1934 'MacRobertson' race from England to Australia was sponsored by Australian businessman Sir MacPherson Robertson as part of the centennial celebrations of the State of Victoria. It attracted more than seventy entries, of whom twenty actually started and only nine finished, and among them all only one aeroplane was designed specifically to compete in the race. At the beginning of 1934 de Havilland announced that, provided orders were received by the end of February (the race was to start on 20 October), it would design and build a special racing aircraft for £5,000 (about half the true cost).

Three customers came forward: James and Amy Mollison, sportsman Bernard Rubin, and hotelier A. O. Edwards; and, true to their word, de Havilland had the first D.H.88 in the air for its maiden flight on 8 September 1934. It was of all-wood construction, only the engines and landing gear being of metal, and combined for the first time in a British aircraft a retractable landing gear, wing flaps and variable-pitch propellers. The three aircraft were G-ACSP *Black Magic*, flown by the Mollisons; G-ACSR, flown by O. Cathcart-Jones and K. Waller; and G-ACSS *Grosvenor House*, flown by C. W. A. Scott and T. Campbell Black.

The race, which began at 6.30 a.m. from the R.A.F. station at Mildenhall, Suffolk, had five compulsory stopping-places: at Baghdad, Allahabad, Singapore, Darwin and Charleville; the finishing point was at Flemington racecourse, Melbourne, a distance of 11,333 miles (18,239 km) from the start. The Mollisons led all the way to Karachi, but were then delayed by engine and undercarriage troubles, and by Allahabad they had been overtaken by Scott and Black, who (despite some trouble of their own with one engine) went on to reach Melbourne at 3.33 p.m. local time, a total elapsed time of 70 hours 54 minutes 18 seconds at an average flying speed of 158·9 m.p.h. (255·7 km/hr.). Jones and Waller came third in the speed section and fourth overall, and quickly set out on a return flight to set a new out-and-back record of 13 days 6 hours 43 minutes.

Two other Comets were built subsequently, and all five later

**Specification of
de Havilland Comet**

Engines: Two 225 h.p. de Havilland Gipsy Six R in-lines.
Span: 44 ft. 0 in. (14·31 m.).
Length: 29 ft. 0 in. (8·84 m.).
Wing area: 212·5 sq. ft. (19·74 sq. m.).
Take-off weight: 5,320 lb. (2,413 kg.).
Maximum speed: 237 m.p.h. (381 km/hr.).
Service ceiling: 19,000 ft. (5,790 m.).
Maximum range: 2,925 miles (4,707 km.).

made a number of other long-distance flights, though none to rival their performance in the 'MacRobertson'. Scott and Black's G-ACSS is the sole surviving example – and a highly appropriate one – and at the time of writing (1976) was awaiting restoration to full flying condition in the excellent hands of the Shuttleworth Collection at Old Warden aerodrome in Bedfordshire.

38. Junkers Ju 87

In the mid-1940s the McDonnell Aircraft Company in the U.S.A. built a carrier-based jet fighter which it named the Banshee. It is a name that might with considerably greater aptness have been bestowed upon a much less attractive warplane of a decade earlier; but the Junkers Ju 87 gave rise to a name of its own that was to have far more terrifying connotations to millions of Europeans. For the Ju 87 was a Sturzkampfflugzeug, the German word for dive-bomber, and with deadly effect it was to personify the term 'Stuka' for the rest of its career.

Development of the dive-bomber in Germany was fostered by Ernst Udet, after seeing a demonstration by the American Curtiss Helldiver in 1933, and the Ju 87, designed by Dipl. Ing. Hans Pohlmann of Junkers, made its first flight in the late spring of 1935. Even today it would still be in any 'top ten' awards for ugliness, but then beauty was hardly its business. To put it as generously as possible, its design was strictly functional, and there is no doubt that this objective was achieved.

The initial Ju 87A version, blooded in the Spanish Civil War from December 1937, was soon superseded by the improved Ju 87B with (though it may not have looked like it) aerodynamic improvements and a substantially more powerful engine. Able to carry up to 1,000 kg. of bombs, according to version, the Ju 87B also was fitted with small sirens near the tops of the main undercarriage leg fairings, to add a devastating and demoralising scream to the whine of its engine and the whistle of its falling bombs.

Hailed as the 'supreme weapon' by the German propaganda machine, it did indeed appear to justify this title as it screamed and bombed its way through Poland, Norway, France and the Low Countries during

World War 2, against little or no effective fighter opposition. Then, at Dunkirk and in the Battle of Britain, it came up against the Hurricane and Spitfire – and was quickly proved to be clumsy, poorly armed and extremely vulnerable. Before the end of August 1940 it had been withdrawn from major operations against Britain, though later, in conditions more favourable to it, it succeeded again in Greece, in Crete and on the Russian Front. But the 'supreme weapon' myth had by then been exploded, and even its quite successful use as a tank-buster (Ju 87D) and anti-shipping aircraft (Ju 87R) was not enough to fully restore its tarnished reputation.

Specification of
Junkers Ju 87A-1
Engine: One 600 h.p. Junkers Jumo 210Ca inverted-Vee type.
Span: 45 ft. 3⅓ in. (13·80 m.).
Length: 35 ft. 5¼ in. (10·80 m.).
Wing area: 343·4 sq. ft. (31·90 sq. m.).
Maximum take-off weight: 7,496 lb. (3,400 kg.).
Maximum speed with 250 kg. bomb: 183 m.p.h. (295 km/hr.) at 9,850 ft. (3,000 m.).
Service ceiling: 22,965 ft. (7,000 m.).
Maximum range: 621 miles (1,000 km.).

---

39. North American Texan/Harvard

It has been claimed that more pilots have learned to fly on variants of the North American Texan (R.A.F. Harvard) than on any other type of aircraft, and such a claim would be difficult to refute, since the whole family of these tandem two-seat trainers amassed a production total of more than 17,000 aircraft. They were all sired by the fixed-undercarriage NA-16 of 1935, which was designed by R. H. Rice and went into service with the U.S. Army Air Corps as the BT-9 Yale and the U.S. Navy as the NJ-1. In 1937 another U.S.A.A.C. competition yielded the NA-26, which in turn was to become the BC-1 (Navy SNJ-1) and later the AT-6 Texan, with higher-powered engine and retractable landing gear.

In June 1938, as part of the R.A.F. Expansion Scheme, the Texan was one of the first American types to be ordered by the British Purchasing Commission, and deliveries of these (as the Harvard I) began at the end of that year. Others followed under Lend-Lease, and altogether more than 5,000 were supplied for training Allied air forces during World War 2, these being of successively later marks with square-cut wingtips, straight-backed rudders and other refinements. A well-known wartime cartoon has two servicemen, with hands over their ears, saying as a four-engined bomber zooms low overhead: 'Another of those perishing Harvards!'; and it is certainly true that noise was a prominent characteristic of the type, created by the high tip speed of its direct-drive propeller.

Service with the Royal Air Force continued, in fact, until March 1955 in the training role, and thereafter Harvards were used on other duties against the Mau-Mau in Kenya and terrorists in Malaya. Production of

both fixed and retractable gear versions took place also in Australia (as the Wirraway trainer and Ceres crop-duster), Canada (Harvard), Japan and Sweden; and the Texan has appeared in numerous guises, from light attack aircraft to private racer. But it is as a basic trainer that it will always be remembered, ranking with those other great 'flying classrooms', the Avro 504, Curtiss Jenny and de Havilland Tiger Moth.

40. Boeing Flying Fortress

The Flying Fortress was so named by Boeing to indicate its original purpose, which was that of defending the U.S. homeland by acting as an anti-shipping bomber in home waters – a role, incidentally, allocated to the U.S. Army Air Corps in the mid-1930s, much to the disgust of the Navy. Instead, circumstances caused it to become the spearhead, with its no less illustrious contemporary, the Liberator, of the United States' daylight bombing offensive against Nazi Germany in 1942–45.

For a 'fortress', Boeing's Model 299 prototype which first flew on 28 July 1935, was but lightly defended, a fact that was quickly and effectively remedied

---

Specification of North American Texan

Engine: One 600 h.p. Pratt & Whitney R-1340-49 Wasp radial.
Span: 42 ft. 0 in. (12·80 m.).
Length: 29 ft. 0 in. (8·84 m.).
Wing area: 254·0 sq. ft. (23·60 sq. m.).
Take-off weight: 5,155 lb. (2,338 kg.).
Maximum speed: 210 m.p.h. (338 km/hr.).
Service ceiling: 24,200 ft. (7,375 m.).
Range: 629 miles (1,013 km.).

during World War 2 when the five machine-guns of the original B-17B were increased to seven in the B-17C, nine in the B-17E, thirteen in the B-17F, and a maximum of fourteen in the B-17G. This last-mentioned model accounted for some two-thirds of the 12,731 Flying Fortresses built by Boeing and others, and it is a measure of America's wartime production capability, that, whereas only 631 B-17s were built between 1938 and 1941, the total rose to 12,085 between 1942 and 1945.

At the peak, in mid-1944, Boeing's Seattle plant was alone turning out sixteen B-17Gs every twenty-four hours. The Model 299 prototype showed its capabilities at a very early date, when it completed its delivery flight in August 1935 from Seattle to Wright Field, Dayton, Ohio – a distance of 2,100 miles (3,380 km) – at an average speed of more than 232 m.p.h. (373 km/hr.); and in 1938–39 there were numerous other impressive long-distance flights.

In August 1939 one of the service trials aircraft, with supercharged engines, lifted an 11,000 lb. (4,990 kg) payload to an altitude of 34,000 ft. (10,363 m.) and set a 1,000 km (621 mile) closed circuit speed record of 259·4

m.p.h. (417·5 km/hr.). That this level of performance was not eroded under operational conditions can be seen by reference to the data given below.

Apart from its ability to maintain performance at height, perhaps the Fortress's other major attribute was the degree of adaptability that is inherent in most well-designed aeroplanes; adaptability not only in a structural sense – the B-17E, for example, embodied some 30 per cent redesign compared with earlier models – but in the operational sense as well. Such versatility enabled the Fortress to perform, during World War 2 and after, not only as a superb

---

**Specification of
B-17G Flying Fortress**

Engines: Four 1,200 h.p. Wright R-1820-97 Cyclone radials.
Span: 103 ft. 9⅜ in. (31·63 m.).
Length: 74 ft. 8¾ in. (22·78 m.).
Wing area: 1,420·0 sq. ft. (131·92 sq. m.).
Normal take-off weight: 55,000 lb. (24,948 kg.).
Normal maximum speed: 287 m.p.h. (462 km/hr.) at 25,000 ft. (7,620 m.).
Service ceiling: 35,600 ft. (10,850 m.).
Normal maximum range: 1,800 miles (2,897 km.).

---

bomber but as photo-reconnaissance aircraft, maritime patroller (at last!), air/sea rescue aircraft, flying bomb, and even as a stop-gap airliner.

41. Martin M-130

'Captain Musick, you have your sailing orders. Cast off and depart for Manila in accordance therewith.' With these words the U.S. Postmaster-General, James Farley, climaxed the departure of NC14716 *China Clipper*, a giant Martin flying-boat, on the first scheduled air-mail flight across the Pacific. On board, in addition to the crew of seven, were 110,000 letters bound for the *Clipper*'s stopping-places at Honolulu, Midway, Wake, Guam and Manila, and beyond.

Departing from San Francisco Bay at 3.46 p.m. Pacific Standard Time, *China Clipper* had a tumultuous send-off from a 25,000-strong crowd, fireworks, whistles, sirens, and an overhead flying display. She alighted at Manila at 3.32 p.m. local time on 29 November – two minutes late – and made the return trip between 2 and 6 December, having covered some 16,420 miles (26,425 km) at an average flying speed of 133·2 m.p.h. (214·4 km/hr.). She was 6 hours 48 minutes inside the schedule allowed, had set nineteen records en route, and had achieved it all without any 'pushing' and with no delays due to weather or maintenance problems.

In a subsequent nine-year career of around 20,000 flying hours, during which time she covered some three million miles (4·83 million km), *China Clipper* is still best remembered for that one inaugural flight. She had flown for the first time on 30 December 1934, one of three Martin M-130s designed for Pan American by a team under Lassiter Milburn and built between 1933 and 1935. Her sister 'boats, *Hawaii Clipper* and *Philippine Clipper*, joined her in service shortly afterwards, at first flying air-mail services and then, from 21 October 1936, scheduled passenger services across the Pacific.

Accommodation was for up to thirty-six day passengers, in three eight-person cabins with a 12-person lounge/dining-room between; or, on night schedules, six double or twelve single sleeping berths. Sadly, none of the three *Clippers* survive. *Hawaii* was lost without trace between Guam and Manila on 28 July

1938, then with a total of 4,808 flying hours to her credit. *Philippine*, having fortunately departed from Wake Island two days before the Japanese attack on Pearl Harbor, joined *China* in temporary U.S. Navy service in 1942, but after returning to Pan Am service went off course and crashed in California on 21 January 1943. She had then accumulated 14,628 flying hours. *China Clipper*, having also returned to PanAm, was placed on the service from Miami to Leopoldville, but crashed at Port of Spain, Trinidad, on 8 January 1945, after striking an unlit boat during a night landing.

Specification of Martin M-130

Engines: Four 830 h.p. Pratt & Whitney R-1830-S1A4G Twin Wasp radials.
Span: 130 ft. 0 in. (39·62 m.).
Length: 90 ft. 7½ in. (27·62 m.).
Wing area: 2,315·0 sq. ft. (215·07 sq. m.), including sponsons.
Take-off weight: 52,000 lb. (23,587 kg.).
Maximum cruising speed: 163 m.p.h. (262 km/hr.) at 7,000 ft. (2,135 m.).
Service ceiling: 17,000 ft. (5,182 m.).
Range: 3,200 miles (5,150 km.).

---

42.   Messerschmitt Bf 109

An overall figure for production of all variants of the Messerschmitt Bf 109 is virtually impossible to determine, but it is reasonably safe to assert that it was of the order of at least 34,000 – in other words, approximately equal to the *combined* output of its great wartime opponents, the Hurricane and Spitfire, and thereby one of the most extensively produced aircraft of all time. Its final version, the Bf 109G, was alone built in numbers comparable to those of the Hurricane. Moreover the Bf 109, unlike its British contemporaries, remained basically a fighter or fighter-bomber all its operational life, apart from a few unprofitable excursions into other potential roles.

It preceded the Hurricane by about a year, gaining its first RLM contract in 1933 and making its maiden flight in early September 1935 – powered, as irony would have it, by a British engine, the Rolls-Royce Kestrel V. This, however, was only because of the non-availability of the Junkers Jumo 210, which was introduced in later prototypes and in the Bf 109B initial production series. First operational experience was gained in

1937 with Jagdgruppe 88 of the Condor Legion in Spain, and in the same year the Bf 109B entered service at home with the celebrated 'Richthofen' Geschwader. That year was also notable for the world absolute speed record of 379·38 m.p.h. (610·55 km/hr.) set up by the thirteenth prototype on 11 November.

This was a specially prepared aircraft with a boosted Daimler-Benz DB 601 engine, and it was this power plant that eventually became the definitive engine for the 109. It was introduced into service in the Bf 109E series, which began to reach Luftwaffe fighter units at the beginning of 1939 and which formed the substantive service version right through the Battle of Britain. Superior in speed to the Hurricane at all altitudes, and faster in both climb and dive, the Bf 109E could, moreover, approximately match the Spitfire I in these areas, though it could be out-turned by both British fighters. But its very short tactical radius, leaving it fuel for only about 20 minutes combat once arriving over southern England, put it at a considerable disadvantage, and in the four months July–October 1940 the number of Bf 109s lost or damaged – not all due to combat – reached some 877.

Best of all variants was the Bf 109F, in which the 'F' might well have stood for 'face-lift', for it had a 1,200 or 1,300 h.p. engine, improved nose contours, extended-span round-tipped wings, cantilever tailplane and retractable tailwheel, and was the first version able to out-climb the Spitfire V. In the late summer of 1942 it was supplanted by the Bf 109G; but the peak of performance had been passed, and this version, despite its more powerful DB 605 engine, was so much heavier that its performance was in fact poorer than the F. Post-war production of the Messerschmitt 109 took place in Czechoslovakia and Spain, and

---

Specification of Messerschmitt Bf 109F-2

Engine: One 1,200 h.p. Daimler-Benz DB 601N inverted-Vee type.
Span: 32 ft. 5¾ in. (9·90 m.).
Length: 29 ft. 0⅛ in. (8·85 m.).
Wing area: 174·4 sq. ft. (16·20 sq. m.).
Normal take-off weight: 6,173 lb. (2,800 kg.).
Maximum speed: 373 m.p.h. (600 km/hr.) at 19,685 ft. (6,000 m.).
Service ceiling: 36,090 ft. (11,000 m.).
Range with under-fuselage drop-tank: 528 miles (850 km.).

the type continued in service for some years after the end of hostilities in Europe.

43. Hawker Hurricane

Well named was Sydney Camm's Hurricane, for it undoubtedly brought a forceful wind of change blowing down the Air Staff corridors in Whitehall, and was the forerunner of the equally gusty Typhoon, Tornado and Tempest of later years. It was, equally certainly, the right aeroplane at the right time, for the first steps which led to its eventual production took place in the same year that a certain Herr Hitler came to power in Germany. Ostensibly, its design began in the following year, to Air Ministry Specification F.36/34, and a successful first flight on 6 November 1935 was followed by the achievement on test of a speed of 315 m.p.h. (507 km/hr.) in level flight. But not only was the Hurricane the first British fighter to exceed 300 m.p.h. (483 km/hr.); it was, in addition, the first to feature a fully-enclosed cockpit and fully-retractable landing gear, and the first to carry an eight-gun armament. But above all it was a monoplane, and its acceptance by the R.A.F. signified at last the service's escape from 'biplanitis'.

So confident were Hawkers of receiving substantial orders for the new fighter that they began to prepare in March 1936 for the production of up to 1,000 of them. That confidence was not misplaced: three months later came an initial contract for 600 – the largest for any British warplane since World War I – and the eventual total of Hurricanes built reached 14,533. Just over 300 of these were in service at the outbreak of war, and Hawker's foresight stood England in good stead when the Battle of Britain began in the summer of 1940, for Hurricanes outnumbered Spitfires in service by about 2 to 1.

The Hurricane had, in fact, been blooded in France in the preceding months, with particularly heavy losses (nearly 400) during the period from 10 May to 20 June, mainly to the Messerschmitt 109E, which it could not out-run or out-climb. In theory, at least, the Hurricane's main task during the Battle of Britain was to engage the enemy bombers, leaving the fighters to the faster Spitfire; but in practice it had plenty of fighter *v.* fighter combat, and provided the enemy aircraft could be denied a height advantage the Hurricane was well able to out-turn and out-manoeuvre the 109, as the latter's loss rate can testify. Moreover, as well as being a good gun platform, it was a good 'production' aeroplane – easy to build and easy to repair, so ensuring that replacements could keep pace with combat losses.

From 1942 it began also to show another virtue: versatility, becoming a ground attack and anti-tank fighter-bomber and a sea-going catapult fighter for convoy protection. It is perhaps remarkable that only one Victoria Cross was awarded to a Fighter Command pilot during the whole of the war; but it is indisputably fitting that that officer – Flt Lt J. B. Nicolson of No. 249 Squadron – should have earned it for a Hurricane action during the Battle of Britain.

44. Supermarine Spitfire

Air Ministry Specification F.7/30 was a fairly rigid one, but to Reginald Mitchell, designer of the successful S.4/S.5/S.6 series of Schneider Trophy seaplanes, the production of a fighter capable of 250 m.p.h. (402 km/hr.) can scarcely have seemed an impossible challenge. Yet the fighter which Supermarine built to that specification – an open-cockpit monoplane with a thick, gull wing, fixed 'trousered' undercarriage and the wretched steam-cooled Rolls-Royce Goshawk engine – fell short of even that relatively modest target by a full 20 m.p.h. (32 km/hr.).

Fortunately for all except the Axis powers in World War 2, Mitchell decided also to design another fighter as a private venture to his own specification, to show what could really be done. His prototype, later to become the legendary Spitfire, made its first flight on 5 March 1936 and was later clocked in tests at a level speed of 349·5 m.p.h.

Specification of Hawker Hurricane prototype

Engine: One 990 h.p. Rolls-Royce Merlin C Vee-type.
Span: 40 ft. 0 in. (12·19 m.).
Length: 31 ft. 6 in. (9·60 m.).
Wing area: 257·5 sq. ft. (23·92 sq. m.).
Take-off weight: 5,670 lb. (2,572 kg.).
Maximum speed: 315 m.p.h. (507 km/hr.) at 16,200 ft. (4,940 m.).
Service ceiling: 34,000 ft. (10,365 m.).
Maximum range: 525 miles (845 km.).

(562·5 km/hr.). Two days before the first flight, on the same date that it had ordered 600 Hurricanes from Hawker, the Air Ministry had placed another contract, with Supermarine, for 310 examples of Mitchell's fighter. The prototype made a fleeting fly-past at the Hendon R.A.F. Display later that month, but – like the prototype Hurricane – was to be the only example of its kind in existence for the next two years.

The first production Spitfire was delivered in August 1938, and by the outbreak of World War 2 some 4,000 were on order for the R.A.F. Production continued until October 1947, by which time more than 22,700 Spitfires and 'navalised' Seafires had been completed, in nearly thirty different models. Nineteen Spitfire-equipped squadrons took part in the Battle of Britain in 1940, most of these being Mks I/IA/IB with a few Mk IIAs in the later stages. To detail all the different versions would take – and, indeed, frequently has taken – a full-length book, but two or three milestones of Spitfire progress may be mentioned as typical.

In 1931, Mitchell's ultimate Schneider Trophy seaplane, the S.6B, had set a world speed record of 406·94 m.p.h. (654·9 km/hr.), thereby becoming the first aeroplane in the world to exceed 400 m.p.h. (644 km/hr.). The first Spitfire to exceed the 400 m.p.h. figure was the Mk VII (416 m.p.h.; 669·5 km/hr.); first to introduce the more powerful Griffon engine in place of the Merlin was the Mk XII; among the most successful Griffon versions was the Mk XIV, used against the V-1 flying bombs and one of the first Allied aircraft to destroy an Me 262 jet fighter in combat; and the fastest Spitfire of all was the F.22, capable of a maximum speed of 455 m.p.h. (732 km/hr.).

Of the Spitfire it can truly be

Specification of Supermarine Spitfire I

Engine: One 1,030 h.p. Rolls-Royce Merlin II Vee-type.
Span: 36 ft. 10 in. (11·23 m.).
Length: 29 ft. 11 in. (9·12 m.).
Wing area: 242·0 sq. ft. (22·48 sq. m.).
Normal take-off weight: 6,200 lb. (2,812 kg.).
Maximum speed: 362 m.p.h. (583 km/hr.) at 19,000 ft. (5,790 m.).
Service ceiling: 31,900 ft. (9,725 m.).
Range: 395 miles (636 km.).

said that it became a legend in its own lifetime. Sadly, it was a triumphant life that its designer did not live to see, for Reginald Mitchell died on 11 June 1937, a victim of cancer at the early age of 42; but what a legacy he left behind.

45. Mitsubishi Karigane

The national prestige accruing from spectacular flights – particularly international ones – was something sought by many countries in the 1920s and 1930s, before international air travel became as commonplace as it is today. To Britain, the natural objectives for long-distance flights were the far-flung outposts of Empire: South Africa, India and Australia; or (in common with other European nations) across the Atlantic to North and South America. Conversely, England herself was a natural choice when Japan decided to enter into the spirit of things.

In 1937 the Asahi Shimbun newspaper group in Tokyo foresaw the chance of a doubly-spectacular news story if it could not only sponsor an endurance flight to London but also, on the return trip, have photographs brought back to Japan of the Coronation of King George VI. The aeroplane chosen was the second prototype of the Mitsubishi Ki-15, a two-seat high-speed reconnaissance aircraft then beginning production for the Army Air Force, which in civil guise became known as the Karigane I (Wild Goose).

Registered J-BAAI, this prototype was delivered to Asahi in late March 1937, and at 5.12 p.m. (G.M.T.) on Monday, 5 April, it took off from Tachikawa airfield near Tokyo on the first stage of its journey. It finally touched down at Croydon at 3.30 p.m. (G.M.T.) on the following Friday, an elapsed time of 94 hours 17 minutes 56 seconds for the 9,542 mile (15,357 km) journey, covered at an average speed of 101·193 m.p.h. (162·854 km/hr.). Actual flying time was 51 hours 19 minutes 23 seconds.

Designed under the leadership of Fumihiko Kono, the original Ki-15 prototype had made its first flight in May 1936. The Tokyo–London aeroplane, named *Kamikaze* (Divine Wind), was flown by Masaaki Iinuma, with Kenji Tsukagoshi as navigator/radio operator. Between 14 and 25 May 1937, at about the time the first Ki-15s were being delivered to Japanese AAF squadrons, the *Kamikaze* flew a more southerly and more leisurely return trip to Tokyo with its collection of Coronation photographs. At that time, no one could have foreseen that, within five or six years, British pilots would be at war with the Karigane's lineal descendant, the 'Zero' fighter; or that, for the Western world, the word *Kamikaze* would have taken on a new and far more deadly meaning.

Specification of Mitsubishi Karigane

Engine: One 550 h.p. Nakajima Ha 8 Kotobuki 3 radial.
Span: 39 ft. 4⅞ in. (12·01 m.).
Length: 28 ft. 0¾ in. (8·552 m.).
Wing area: 258·3 sq. ft. (24·00 sq. m.).
Take-off weight: 5,071 lb. (2,300 kg.).
Maximum speed: 311 m.p.h. (500 km/hr.).
Range: 1,491 miles (2,400 km.).

---

46. Short 'C' class

Bring together a carefully worked out specification, an ingenious designer and a thoroughly reliable power plant, and the result will very seldom fail to produce a pretty good aeroplane.

Nevertheless, Imperial Airways were considered to be taking quite a gamble when, in 1935, they decided to spend £1¾ million – a sum that today would just about buy half a Phantom – on a fleet of twenty-eight brand-new flying-boats before a prototype had even flown.

The reason was the 1934 Empire Air Mail Scheme, whereby all mail between countries of the British Empire was to be carried without a surcharge. The specification, drawn up by Imperial's Technical Adviser, Major R. H. Mayo, was for an aircraft able to carry twenty-four passengers and 1½ tons of mail or other freight, cruise at 160 m.p.h. (257·5 km/hr.) and have a normal range of 700 miles (1,126 km). The designer was Arthur Gouge of Short Brothers, and the power plant the Bristol Pegasus nine-cylinder radial.

A flying-boat – a type of which Shorts were one of the world's leading exponents – seemed best suited for the lengthy take-off and landing runs that would be necessary with so large a payload; in his S.23 design, Gouge's three major accomplishments were remarkable spaciousness for the passengers, an excellent length/beam ratio, and area-increasing flaps that gave 30 per cent extra lift for take-off. Indeed, when *Canopus*, the first S.23, made her first flight on 4 July 1936, she 'unstuck' after only 17 seconds. Thirty-five more generally similar 'boats were eventually built for Imperial Airways and all had fleet names beginning with the letter C (hence 'C' class); six others were built for Qantas.

Scheduled services began on 8 February 1937, and by 1938 weekly services were being flown to Egypt (7), East Africa (3), South Africa (2), India (4), Malaya (2) and Australia (2). In a decade of service 1937–47 – for many of them served through and after World War 2 – the 'Empire Boats' flew nearly 38 million miles (61·15 million km); at one stage the air-mail trade was so profitable that the number of passengers was reduced to seventeen and the air-mail payload increased from 3,000 lb. (1,360 kg.) to 4,000 lb. (1,814 kg.). *Caledonia*, a special long-range version with six extra fuel tanks, made a successful Atlantic crossing from Foynes to Botwood on 5–6 July 1937, and in August 1939 there began a regular transatlantic mail service with the flying-boats refuelling in flight from Harrow tankers. The outbreak of World War 2 brought this to a halt; but it also brought into prominence the military descendant of the 'Empire Boats', the no less famous Sunderland.

Specification of Short 'C' class
Engines: Four 920 h.p. Bristol Pegasus Xc radials.
Span: 114 ft. 0 in. (34·75 m.).
Length: 88 ft. 0 in. (26·82 m.).
Wing area: 1,500·0 sq. ft. (139·35 sq. m.).
Take-off weight: 40,500 lb. (18,371 kg.).
Cruising speed: 164 m.p.h. (264 km/hr.).
Absolute ceiling: 20,000 ft. (6,100 m.).
Normal range: 760 miles (1,223 km.).

47. Mitsubishi 'Zero'

'Simplify, and add lightness' has long been one of the aircraft designer's cardinal principles. It has also, traditionally, been particularly hard to accomplish in a carrier-borne combat aircraft, which requires the additional weight of a stronger landing gear, catapult and arrester equipment and other naval impedimenta compared with its land-based brethren. Jiro Horikoshi, in the Mitsubishi A6M Zero-Sen, or Type '0' Navy fighter, achieved both, producing a fighter that was of the order of 1,000 lb. (450 kg.) lighter than the lightest of its early-war opponents, and superbly manoeuvrable.

Here, in contrast to the Short flying-boat situation just related, we have the case of a very tight specification, and an ingenious designer obliged to use a power-plant that he *did not* want. However, with the Nakajima company having withdrawn from the competition, Mitsubishi's was the only contender, and he had little choice but to select the engine that would enable him to meet the specification. The A6M1 prototype was first flown on 1 April 1939, and the A6M2 initial production version was formally accepted by the Imperial Japanese Navy on 31 July 1940.

Curiously, despite its origins, it was as a land-based fighter that the Zero made its operational début. On 19 August 1940 twelve Zeros, escorting Japanese bombers in a raid on Chungking, decimated the opposing Chinese fighters without loss to themselves; indeed, by the end of the year they claimed the destruction of fifty-nine Chinese warplanes, still without the loss of a single Zero. Eight were, however, lost from the seventy-nine

which escorted the bombers attacking Pearl Harbor, and the Zero's success rate against American fighters in the Pacific theatre during the next six months came as a great and disagreeable surprise. (It should not have done so, for they had been warned of the Zero's record in China a year earlier, but chose to disbelieve the reports.)

The tide of the Zeros' fortunes began to turn when they encountered the U.S. F4F Wildcat in early May 1942, in the Battle of the Coral Sea, and they suffered their first serious reverse a month later, at the Battle of Midway. Successive versions, with more power and other improvements, failed fully to restore their edge in performance, but their early reputation for invincibility died hard, and they remained a respected foe throughout the war. Even the slower twin-float version, produced from 1942 to overcome the shortage of land bases, could give a good account of itself against nominally superior opposition. In the final year or so of war the Zero, in common with most other leading Japanese warplanes, was drawn into the *Kamikaze* suicide operations; in fact, the first unit formed specifically for such missions, the Shimpu Special Attack

Corps, was equipped with Zero fighters carrying a 250 kg. bomb under the fuselage. Their first victim, sunk by suicide attack on 25 October 1944, was the American escort carrier *St Lo.*

**Specification of
Mitsubishi A6M2 'Zero'**

Engine: One 940 h.p. Nakajima Sakae 12 radial.
Span: 39 ft. 4½ in. (12·00 m.).
Length: 29 ft. 8¾ in. (9·06 m.).
Wing area: 241·5 sq. ft. (22·44 sq. m.).
Normal take-off weight: 5,313 lb. (2,410 kg.).
Maximum speed: 332 m.p.h. (535 km/hr.) at 14,930 ft. (4,550 m.).
Service ceiling: 32,810 ft. (10,000 m.).
Normal range: 1,162 miles (1,870 km.).

48. Focke-Wulf Fw 190

To Dipl.-Ing. Kurt Tank, one of the most progressive aircraft designers of the past three decades, belongs the distinction of producing what is generally acknowledged as Germany's most successful single-seat fighter of World War 2, the Focke-Wulf Fw 190. By the time the RLM specification for the Fw 190 was

issued, in 1937, the Messerschmitt Bf 109 was well established in production, but the thirty-nine-year-old Tank's design was superior to it in many respects. It was a well-proportioned and aerodynamically clean-looking aircraft, the most noticeable characteristics being a very wide-track main landing gear and a large but neatly cowled B.M.W. 139 radial engine offering 1,550 h.p.

Making its initial flight on 1 June 1939, the first prototype registered a top speed of 370 m.p.h. (595 km/hr.) in subsequent tests, and clearly had great potential. The heavier but more powerful B.M.W. 801 radial was chosen for the initial Fw 190A production series, which entered service with Luftwaffe operational units in 1941. At first used chiefly as a fighter and fighter-bomber, the Fw 190 had a normal armament of four 20 mm. cannon and two 7·9 mm. machine-guns and, at altitudes up to about 20,000 ft. (6,100 m.), could match or improve upon the performance of the Spitfire V, then the best of its Allied adversaries. One of the best of the A series, the Fw 190A-8, could reach a speed of 408 m.p.h. (657 km/hr.) at 20,670 ft. (6,300 m.). Above such heights, however, performance of the Fw 190 began to fall off rapidly, and improvement became an absolute necessity in the face of high-level daytime raids by U.S.A.A.F. bomber formations in the middle war years.

An interim solution was found in the 'Dora' series (Fw 190D), a substantially redesigned version with a 1,750 h.p. Jumo 213A inverted-Vee engine in a lengthened, radial-looking nose. The major D model, the D-9, could reach up to 426 m.p.h. (685 km/hr.) at 21,650 ft. (6,600 m.). But the ultimate 'stretch' appeared in the Ta 152, produced chiefly as a medium (Ta 152C) and high altitude (Ta 152H) fighter, developed from the 'Dora' series.

The former attained 463 m.p.h. (745 km/hr.) at 34,100 ft. (10,400 m.) while the latter, with a boosted engine, could reach no less than 472 m.p.h. (760 km/hr.) at 41,000 ft. (12,500 m.).

Unfortunately, for Germany, the Ta 152 arrived too late and in too small numbers to affect the course of the war. Altogether, some 20,000 aircraft of the Fw 190 family were built, in general maintaining their operational excellence in a variety of roles that also included ground-attack and anti-tank duties.

49. Ilyushin Il-2

Just as the Ju 87 added a new word 'Stuka' to aviation's vocabulary, so a few years later did the Il-2, which became known to the world at large as the 'Stormovik' – an Anglicised form of its military title of Bronirovannyi Shturmovik, or Armoured Ground Attack Aircraft. The Shturmovik was unique. It was also rugged, effective, could be flown by relatively inexperienced crews, and was straightforward to build at a time when it was urgently needed. The 1938 requirement to which it was designed made it essential that

---

Specification of Focke-Wulf Fw 190D-9

Engine: One 1,776 h.p. Junkers Jumo 213 A-1 inverted-Vee type.
Span: 34 ft. 5½ in. (10·50 m.).
Length: 33 ft. 5¼ in. (10·19 m.).
Wing area: 196·98 sq. ft. (18·30 sq. m.).
Normal take-off weight: 9,480 lb. (4,300 kg.).
Maximum speed: 426 m.p.h. (685 km/hr.) at 21,650 ft. (6,600 m.).
Maximum range on internal fuel: 520 miles (837 km.).

it be heavily armoured, but how to achieve this without crippling the performance with excessive weight?

Sergei Ilyushin solved the problem by making the armour an integral part of the structure. The first prototype was flown in the spring of 1939, a production prototype in October 1940, and the first Il-2s became operational in mid-1941, only a few weeks after the Nazi invasion of Russia. These single-seaters, undefended to the rear, proved vulnerable to German fighters, and were superseded by the two-seat Il-2m3, mounting a rearward-firing 12·7 mm. machine-gun in addition to two 23 mm. cannon and two 7·6 mm. machine-guns firing forward. Up to 400 kg. (882 lb.) of bombs and eight 25 kg. (55 lb.) underwing rocket projectiles could be carried, the Il-2 being a pioneer in the introduction of the latter type of weapon.

In action, Il-2s employed three basic tactics: horizontal bombing and strafing at tree-top height, steep-angle dive bombing, and the so-called 'circle of death', in which Il-2s in line astern would cross the lines to one side of their target, circle and attack it from the rear. Tanks, ammunition trains and the like were their particular targets, in which their effectiveness is typified by the battle for Kursk in mid-1943, when the 3rd Panzer Division alone lost 270 out of 300 tanks to Il-2 attacks, in *two hours*, and 2,000 casualties besides.

To the Russians the Il-2 was affectionately 'Ilyusha' or the 'Flying Infantryman'; the Germans had another name for it: Schwarzer Tod – the Black Death. On Christmas Eve 1941, Stalin told factory workers: 'The Red Army needs the Il-2 as much as it needs bread, as much as it needs the air it breathes.' It got them – more than 36,000 of them before, in 1944, it was superseded by the improved Il-10.

Specification of
Ilyushin Il-2m3

Engine: One 1,770 h.p. Mikulin AM-38F Vee-type.
Span: 47 ft. 10¾ in. (14·60 m.).
Length: 38 ft. 2⅝ in. (11·65 m.).
Wing area: 414·4 sq. ft. (38·50 sq. m.).
Normal take-off weight: 12,147 lb. (5,510 kg.).
Maximum speed: 251 m.p.h. (404 km/hr.) at 4,920 ft. (1,500 m.).
Service ceiling: 19,685 ft. (6,000 m.).
Normal range: 373 miles (600 km.).

50. North American Mustang

One hundred days may be a long time in politics, but 120 days is no time at all to design a high-performance fighter, even in the middle of a war. Yet this was the limit set by the British Air Purchasing Commission in April 1940, when seeking an urgent replacement for the Curtiss P-40s then in service with the R.A.F. Designers Raymond Rice and Edgar Schmued bettered the target by three days – even if their NA-73 prototype *was* rolled out on borrowed wheels and still lacked an engine. That engine, when fitted, was an Allison V-1710-39, and with it the prototype made its first flight on 26 October 1940.

A 1,200 h.p. Allison powered the initial production versions for the R.A.F. (Mustang I/IA/II) and U.S.A.A.F. (P-51/P-51A and A-36A), but effectiveness as a fighter was limited by the low altitude rating of the American engine. Even so, the P-51A was no sluggard, with a top speed of 390 m.p.h. (628 km/hr.) at 20,000 ft. (6,100 m.), but in 1942 the introduction of the Rolls-Royce Merlin (licence-built in the U.S.A. by Packard) brought an enormous transformation, allowing the P-51B and Mustang III to reach 440 m.p.h. (708 km/hr.) at 30,000 ft. (9,150 m.).

Pilots loved the new fighter, but did not like the cramping effect of the low cockpit roof, a problem alleviated by the use of the R.A.F. bulged Malcolm hood and then, in the P-51D, by a tear-drop canopy and cut-down rear fuselage giving superb all-round view. The experimental lightweight XP-51F was expressed in production form as the P-51H – too late for World War 2 operations, but the fastest production Mustang, with a maximum speed of 487 m.p.h. (784 km/hr.) at 25,000 ft. (7,620 m.).

But speed and altitude were not the Mustang's only attributes. Produced initially to replace the relatively short-range Tomahawk (P-40), the Mustang was also to become one of the deadliest long-range escort fighters of the war – a valued accompaniment to U.S.A.A.F. bombers both in Europe and the Pacific. In July 1942, when the early Mustangs were just becoming operational with the R.A.F., the British journal *The Aeroplane* reported that: 'Pilots who fly the Mustang praise it so lavishly that they exhaust their superlatives before they have finished their eulogies.'

That that remark still remains true more than thirty years later is attested by the many much-cherished veterans still chasing round the pylons at air races throughout the United States; and American readers must forgive a British writer a touch of chauvinism if he reminds them that it was a British requirement and a British engine that made it all happen.

Specification of North American P-51C

Engine: One 1,695 h.p. Packard-built Rolls-Royce Merlin V-1650-7 Vee-type.
Span: 37 ft. 0¼ in. (11·28 m.).
Length: 32 ft. 3 in. (9·83 m.).
Wing area: 233·0 sq. ft. (21·65 sq. m.).
Take-off weight: 9,800 lb. (4,445 kg.).
Maximum speed: 439 m.p.h. (706·5 km/hr.) at 25,000 ft. (7,620 m.).
Service ceiling: 41,900 ft. (12,770 m.).
Normal range: 950 miles (1,529 km.).

---

51. de Havilland Mosquito

In the D.H.98 Mosquito, de Havilland offered the Royal Air Force what Hawker had offered it a decade earlier with the Hart – a bomber aircraft with a top speed high enough for it to outrun most fighters then in service; a bomber, moreover, so certain of being able to do so that it carried no defensive armament. Power and weight were the keys to this: the power of the Rolls-Royce Merlin engine, and the light structural weight made possible by the adoption of a wooden semi-monocoque airframe instead of a metal one, a formula already tried and proved with no little success on the D.H.88 Comet racer and D.H.91 Albatross airliner.

Conceived in 1938, the D.H.98 did not immediately excite the Air Staff into action, but eventually, in March 1940, they placed an order for fifty, and the first of these flew on 25 November the same year. These fifty were, in fact, divided into three batches, ten each being completed as bombers and photographic reconnaissance aircraft and the other thirty as night fighters. In 1940, with the imminence of the 'blitz', these priorities seemed about right. R.A.F. operational units, to whom the first few Mosquitos were delivered in July 1941, also were a little dubious at first, not sure how 'all that plywood and glue' would withstand the rigours and damage of battle.

They need not have worried; before long, the Mosquito was instead being hailed as 'The Wooden Wonder'. Less emotively, it was a 'high-performance multi-purpose military monoplane', a term which, though accurate enough, did less than justice to a superbly adaptable aeroplane: during its wartime and post-war career the Mosquito performed as day fighter, night fighter, fighter-bomber, high-speed day bomber, pathfinder, night interdictor, photographic aircraft, torpedo fighter, ground-attack aircraft, mail and freight carrier, trainer, and target tug.

It carried bombs of up to 4,000 lb. in size, a variety of guns of calibres up to the six-pounder 57 mm. cannon shown in the colour illustration, underwing rocket projectiles, cameras, and various radars. Nearly 7,800 were built, and Merlin engines were fitted throughout well over thirty different variants. The prototype, W4050, is one of some two dozen Mosquitos to survive, and is on display at Salisbury Hall, Hertfordshire, where it was built in 1940.

Specification of Mosquito F.B. XVIII

Engines: Two 1,635 h.p. Rolls-Royce Merlin 25 Vee-type.
Span: 54 ft. 2 in. (16·51 m.).
Length: 40 ft. 9½ in. (12·43 m.).
Wing area: 454·0 sq. ft. (42·18 sq. m.).
Take-off weight: 22,764 lb. (10,325 kg.).
Performance data for F.B.VI at take-off weight of 19,500 lb. (8,845 kg.):
Maximum speed: 380 m.p.h. (611 km/hr.) at 13,000 ft. (3,960 m.).
Service ceiling: 33,000 ft. (10,060 m.).
Range: 1,650 miles (2,655 km.).

---

52. Avro Lancaster

Avro's twin-engined bomber of the early World War 2 years, the Manchester, was a victim of its unsuccessful Rolls-Royce Vulture engine; its successor, the Lancaster, became, in the (admittedly partisan) view of Air Chief Marshal 'Bomber' Harris, 'the greatest single factor' in winning World War 2. It was the aircraft which, more than any other, enabled the R.A.F. to carry the war to the German homeland, and, if the award of eleven Victoria Crosses to its crew members is any criterion, the Air Marshal certainly had a point.

First flown (as the Manchester III) on 9 January 1941, it began its operational career unspectacularly enough, on the night of 2–3 March 1942, by laying mines in the Heligoland Bight. Lancasters from five Bomber Command squadrons were among the 1,046 aircraft launched against Cologne in Operation Millennium, the first 'thousand-bomber' raid. By the end of the war nearly 7,400 Lancasters had been built, and no fewer than fifty-six Bomber Command squadrons had been equipped with them.

The undoubted highlights of a busy career were the breaching of the Ruhr dams by No. 617 Squadron on the night of 17–18 May 1943; the attacks on the battleship *Tirpitz* in 1944, with her eventual sinking in Tromso Fjord, Norway, on 12 November that year; and the destruction of the great Bielefeld Viaduct in Germany on 14 March 1945. It is no coincidence that each of these involved the use of a special type of bomb, for its adaptability to carry these unusual weapons was one of the keys to the Lancaster's success. Designed originally to carry bombs of up to 4,000 lb. in size,

the Lancaster lent itself equally to Barnes Wallis's 'skipping bomb' used in the dams raid, the 12,000 lb. 'Tallboy' which sank the *Tirpitz*, and the gigantic 22,000 lb. 'Grand Slam' bomb which shattered the Bielefeld Viaduct.

Today there are little more than a dozen Lancasters left around the world, and approximately half of these are Canadian B.Xs, of which Victory Aircraft Ltd. of Toronto built 430. One of these, which forms the subject of the colour illustration, was acquired by Sir William Roberts for his Strathallan Aircraft Collection in Scotland, and in 1975 he approached British Caledonian Airways for technical advice on bringing it back to Britain. The airline went one better – they offered to provide a crew and fly it home for him. Between 16–20 May 1975 a crew comprising Capts Alec Mackenzie and Gerry Moore (pilot and co-pilot), David Kemp (navigator) and Stanley Banfield (flight engineer) ferried it back from Edmonton to Glasgow via Toronto, Halifax, Gander and Reykjavik, a journey of some 5,500 miles (8,850 km). It was delivered to Strathallan airfield on 11 June 1975. During the previous ten years this aircraft had flown only 16 hours, and had not flown at all between 1972 and 1975; despite which, as Capt Mackenzie recorded later, 'the whole aircraft performed marvellously and never gave us a really anxious moment'. No pilot can ask more than that.

Specification of Avro Lancaster B.X

Engines: Four 1,640 h.p. Rolls-Royce Merlin 224 Vee-type.
Span: 102 ft. 0 in. (31·09 m.).
Length: 68 ft. 10 in. (20·98 m.).
Wing area: 1,297·0 sq. ft. (119·49 sq. m.).
Maximum take-off weight: 61,500 lb. (27,896 kg.).
Maximum speed: 250 m.p.h. (402 km/hr.) at 11,000 ft. (3,350 m.).
Service ceiling: 19,000 ft. (5,790 m.).
Typical range: 2,250 miles (3,620 km.).

---

53. Messerschmitt Me 262

The Me 262, the one combat aircraft with which Germany might have been able to regain her lost air supremacy in 1943–45, began to take shape on the Messerschmitt company's drawing-boards in 1938, a full year before the outbreak of World War 2. It was submitted to the German Air Ministry, as Project 1065, on 7 June 1939, and three prototypes were ordered in the following March. By the time the first of these was completed, its turbojet engines were still awaited, and so, to test the airframe, the first Me 262 was fitted with dummy jet engine nacelles under the wings and a 1,200 h.p. Jumo 210G piston engine in the nose; in this form it flew for the first time on 18 April 1941.

The originally intended jet engines, B.M.W. 003s, were fitted to the second aircraft, and both suffered turbine blade failure immediately after the first take-off on 25 March 1942; fortunately the Jumo engine was just about able to bring it down safely. The first all-jet take-off, this time with Jumo 004 engines, did not occur until 18 July 1942. It then took another two years before the Me 262 flew its first operational sortie, a delay occasioned by three basic factors.

Much has been made of Hitler's personal interference, and his demands that priority be given to production of this high-speed jet interceptor for a bombing role. Also, no doubt, the depredations caused by Allied bombing, on the Messerschmitt factories in particular, played their part. But even without either of these contributing factors it is highly improbable that the protracted development of the Me 262's Jumo 004 engines would have enabled the aircraft to enter Luftwaffe service very much sooner.

It eventually did so with a test unit, Erprobungskommando 262, with whom it first fired its guns in anger on 25 July 1944, two days before No. 616 Squadron flew *its* first operational sortie with the R.A.F.'s first jet fighter, the Gloster Meteor – an 'Operation Diver' mission against a V-1 flying bomb. Curiously, the two jet fighters never met in combat during World War 2, most Me 262s that were shot down falling

---

Specification of Messerschmitt Me 262B

Engines: Two 1,984 lb. (900 kg.) s.t. Junkers Jumo 109–004 B-1 turbojets.
Span: 40 ft. 11½ in. (12·48 m.).
Length: 34 ft. 11¼ in. (10·65 m.).
Wing area: 233·8 sq. ft. (21·72 sq. m.).
Take-off weight: approx. 15,432 lb. (7,000 kg.).
Maximum speed: approx. 503 m.p.h. (810 km/hr.) at 19,685 ft. (6,000 m.).
Service ceiling: 34,450 ft. (10,500 m.).
Range: 559 miles (900 km.).

---

to Allied Spitfires, Tempests, Mustangs and Thunderbolts – all piston-engined. Probably only 200 or so Me 262s actually saw service, although just over 1,400 were built by the war's end. Their undoubted technical excellence was matched with effective operational ability in the hands of an experienced fighter pilot such as Oberstleutnant Heinz Bär, who scored 16 of his 220 wartime victories in the Me 262.

54. Lockheed Constellation

Once described as the 'secret weapon' among post-war U.S. transport aircraft, the Constellation was, in fact, designed in 1939, after Lockheed had been requested to design for T.W.A. an aircraft superior to the Douglas DC-4. The outbreak of war nullified this requirement, but eventual notice was taken of the design by the U.S.A.A.F., which ordered a small quantity as C-69 transports, and one of these made the first flight on 9 January 1943; but it was in the immediate post-war period that the 'Connie' made its biggest impact.

To meet their original brief, Lockheed designers Hall Hibbard and Clarence ('Kelly') Johnson had given the Constellation a pressurised fuselage, powerful engines, reversible-pitch propellers, hydraulically-boosted powered controls and Fowler-type landing flaps; the wings were in essence, a scale-up of those on the Lockheed P-38 Lightning fighter, and the fuselage in profile was as near as possible to an ideal aerofoil shape. Drag characteristics were markedly better than those of the DC-4, despite a near-identical frontal area, and early tests had indicated favourably that attribute much loved by airline operators – growth potential.

All of which lends credence to the story that the name 'Constellation' was chosen because the dictionary defined it as 'an assemblage of splendours or excellences'. Be that as it may, the first Constellations went into service almost simultaneously in February 1946 with Pan American and T.W.A., carrying up to forty-eight passengers. (The original specification had said forty.) Later that year Lockheed introduced the 'gold plate' Model 649, so called because of its plusher passenger accommodation, and in 1947 the Model 749 with extra fuel. Soon the Connie was holder of an enviable treble 'first': the first post-war airliner to make scheduled non-stop coast-to-coast flights across the

United States; the first to fly regularly non-stop across the North Atlantic; and the first to operate a right-round-the-world service.

The aircraft shown in the colour plate is fitted with a ventral 'Speedpak', a special flush-fitting container, reducing speed by only 12 m.p.h. (19 km/hr.), which could hold 8,200 lb. (3,720 kg.) of mail or freight. But this device was short-lived, for more growth potential was on the way in the shape of the Model 1049 Super Constellation. First flown on 13 October 1950, it was 18 ft. 4 in. (5·59 m.) longer, had more fuel, more powerful engines, and could

---

Specification of Lockheed Constellation

Engines: Four 2,500 h.p. Wright GR-3350-C18-BD1 Cyclone radials.
Span: 123 ft. 0 in. (37·49 m.).
Length: 95 ft. $1\frac{3}{16}$ in. (28·99 m.).
Wing area: 1,650·0 sq. ft. (153·29 sq. m.).
Maximum take-off weight: 94,000 lb. (42,638 kg.).
Maximum cruising speed: 320 m.p.h. (515 km/hr.).
Service ceiling: 25,000 ft. (7,620 m.).
Maximum range: 4,630 miles (7,450 km.).

carry more passengers a greater distance. Successively improved Supers were followed six years later by the ultimate model, the seventy-five-passenger Starliner, 2 ft. 7 in. (0·79 m.) longer still and with a new 150 ft. (45·72 m.) wing holding even more fuel. By then, however, the Connie's days were numbered: within two more years the great jet airliner scramble was to begin.

55. Bell X-1

'I've tried to think back to that first flight past Mach 1, but it doesn't seem any more important than any of the others. I was kind of disappointed that it wasn't more of a big charge than it was.' Thus, with the understatement typical of the great test pilot, Captain Charles E. ('Chuck') Yeager later recalled his flight in the Bell X-1 on 14 October 1947, when he became the first man successfully to pilot an aeroplane beyond the speed of sound. That flight is now in the record books as 670 m.p.h. (1,078 km/hr.) at 42,000 ft. (12,800 m.), a speed equivalent to Mach 1·015.

The X-1, ordered in 1945 as the XS-1 (S for sonic test), was a joint design by Bell, the U.S.A.A.F. and the N.A.C.A.,

and outwardly was remarkably conventional. Apart from the bullet-shaped fuselage, it had none of the features then considered necessary to pierce the mythical 'sound barrier' – no swept wings, no 'double-wedge' wing section, no power-boosted controls – but it must have been among the first aircraft to have wings machined from solid aluminium alloy, and the airframe was stressed to withstand a staggering 18 g.

It was designed to be air-launched from under the belly of a B-29 or B-50 carrier aircraft, gliding down to a conventional landing after the rocket's fuel was expended, and 46–062, the first of three X-1s, made its first flight – unpowered – on 19 January 1946. The first powered flight followed on 9 December the same year. From January 1949 it made a number of take-offs under its own power. After its last flight, on 12 May 1950, it was handed over to the National Air Museum in Washington.

During its test programme, the X-1 reached 967 m.p.h. (1,556 km/hr.), equivalent to Mach 1·46. Three modified aircraft were ordered in April 1948. These were designated X-1A, X-1B and X-1D; the second X-1 was later redesigned by N.A.C.A. to become the X-1E. These had a stepped cockpit, a longer fuselage housing additional fuel and a turbo-pump system, and the burn time of their rocket motors was increased from 2·5 minutes to 4·2 minutes. In the X-1A, in December 1953, Yeager reached Mach 2·42 at 70,000 ft. (21,340 m.), proving that no further 'barrier' appeared once sonic speed had been passed; and in August 1954 Major Arthur Murray flew it to an altitude of 90,000 ft. (27,430 m.). In each case, the aircraft went out of control after reaching its peak performance, and took no little effort and skill to recover. The

highly-volatile fuel mixture, however, proved even more hazardous than aerodynamic problems, and explosions were to destroy the third X-1 (in 1951), the X-1A (1955) and the X-1D (also 1951). Remarkably, perhaps, the X-1E, which made its first powered flight on 15 December 1955, was the only one of the six to have an ejection seat.

56. Mikoyan/Gurevich MiG-15

That same Artem Mikoyan who had taken part in the production of the ANT-25 had become, by the outbreak of World War 2, the joint leader of the MiG fighter design bureau in partnership with Mikhail Gurevich. Best known of their early products were the wartime MiG-3 and one of Russia's earliest jet fighters, the MiG-9; but it is in later years that the MiG designation has become virtually synonymous with Soviet fighters, and the aircraft which began this great run of success was the MiG-15.

The winner of three competing designs to a 1946 specification, the true prototype was first flown on 30 December 1947, though a more primitive machine

---

**Specification of
Bell X-1A**

Engine: One 6,000 lb. (2,722 kg.) s.t. Reaction Motors XLR-11-RM-5 four-chamber rocket motor.
Span: 28 ft. 0 in. (8·53 m.).
Length: 35 ft. 7 in. (10·85 m.).
Wing area: 130·02 sq. ft. (12·08 sq. m.).
Launching weight: 18,000 lb. (8,165 kg.).
Maximum speed: 1,650 m.p.h. (2,655 km/hr.) at 70,000 ft. (21,325 m.).
Ceiling: 90,000 ft. (27,425 m.).
Endurance: 4·2 minutes at full power.

is said to have flown some five months earlier. It combined the fruits of German and Russian research into swept-back wings, emerging with an anhedral wing with 35 deg. of sweep; but what it really lacked was an adequate engine – though not for long.

With what now seems an incredible lack of foresight, Britain in 1946 had sold twenty-five Rolls-Royce Nene turbojet engines to the Soviet government, and it was not long before this had been developed by Russia into the RD-45 and its successor, the Klimov VK-1, which became the standard powerplant of the MiG-15. The first MiG-15s entered service in 1949, and before the Korean War was very old had presented some nasty surprises to the American F-80 and F-86 pilots of that conflict.

On 8 November 1950 there occurred the first combat 'kill' of one jet fighter by another (won in this case by the F-80C concerned), and by the end of that war in 1953 U.S. fighters had established a marked superiority over the Russian fighter. But the MiG-15 could accelerate, climb and turn faster than the F-86A Sabre, and had a markedly better ceiling. It suf-fered from being a poorer gun platform than the Sabre, having inferior equipment, and most of all from being flown by in-experienced Chinese and North Korean pilots. (Those flown by Russian 'technical advisers' gave a noticeably better account of themselves.)

In short, the MiG-15 was designed for easy mass production and straightforward maintenance, which made it ideal for 'export' to Russia's many less-developed satellites. If Western experts are correct in their estimate that some 15,000 were built (as well as about 9,000 of its more sophisticated successor,

---

Specification of MiG-15bis

Engine: One 5,952 lb. (2,700 kg.) s.t. Klimov VK-1 turbojet.
Span: 33 ft. o¾ in. (10·08 m.).
Length: 33 ft. 1¾ in. (10·10 m.).
Wing area: 221·7 sq. ft. (20·60 sq. m.).
Maximum take-off weight: 12,756 lb. (5,786 kg.).
Maximum speed: 669 m.p.h. (1,076 km/hr.) at 39,375 ft. (12,000 m.).
Service ceiling: 50,850 ft. (15,500 m.).
Maximum range on internal fuel: 1,156 miles (1,860 km.).

the MiG-17), then the MiG-15 holds the record for the world's most extensively built jet aircraft.

57. North American Sabre

A close contemporary of the MiG-15 – it made its first flight some three months earlier, on 1 October 1947 – the Sabre could fairly be said to form the backbone of most Western fighter air arms in the 1950s and early 1960s, just as the Soviet aircraft did for most air forces of the Eastern bloc. The Sabre stemmed from a Navy design, the XFJ-1 Fury, built to a 1944 specification and designed by the same team leaders, Rice and Schmued, who had evolved the Mustang.

Like the Fury, the original XP-86 Sabre began as a straight-winged aircraft; like the MiG-15, it then incorporated German experience of swept wings; and like the MiG-15 it also found 35 deg. the ideal amount of sweep. The first Sabres, for service evaluation, were ordered by the U.S.A.A.F. in December 1946, and on 15 September 1948 one of these set the U.S.A.'s first post-war world air speed record, of 670·981 m.p.h. (1,079·837 km/hr.). That record was to stand for two years before being beaten, in 1952 and again in 1953, by later (F-86D) versions of the same aircraft.

Sabres first encountered the MiG-15 in Korea on 17 December 1950, when four of the Russian fighters were destroyed by F-86As of the 4th Fighter Interception Wing; and the top-scoring jet fighter pilot of that war, with sixteen victories, was another Sabre 'jock': Capt Joseph McConnell Jr. of the 51st F.I. Wing. The 'kill ratio' of the Sabre over the MiG-15 by 1953 was due in the main, as has already been said, to superior equipment (particularly gun-laying equipment) and superior piloting. It was also more strongly built, and was transonic in a shallow dive: on 18 May 1953 it enabled Jacqueline Cochran to become the first woman pilot to exceed the speed of sound.

Korean shortcomings were well taken care of in later models: fastest was the F-86D, at 710 m.p.h. (1,143 km/hr.); longest-ranged, with drop-tanks, was the F-86E, with 705 miles (1,135 km); better manoeuvrability at altitude was conferred in the F-86F by a redesigned wing; best rate of climb (12,000

ft.; 3,658 m./min.) and best
ceiling (55,000 ft.; 16,765 m.)
were offered by the Orenda-
engined Canadair Sabre Mk. 6.

**Specification of
North American F-86F**

Engine: One 5,970 lb. (2,708
kg.) s.t. General Electric
J47-GE-27 turbojet.
Span: 37 ft. 1 in. (11·30 m.).
Length: 37 ft. 6 in. (11·43 m.).
Wing area: 287·9 sq. ft.
(26·75 sq. m.).
Take-off weight: 16,850 lb.
(7,643 kg.).
Maximum speed: 690 m.p.h.
(1,110 km/hr.) at sea level.
Service ceiling: 50,000 ft.
(15,240 m.).
*Combat radius with two
drop-tanks:* 660 miles (1,062
km.).

---

58. Boeing Stratojet

We see in the B-47 Stratojet the
repetition of two themes that
have already become apparent
in this book: the high-speed
bomber that can outpace the
fighters of its day, and the adoption by the victors of World War
2 of the fruits of German wartime experience of swept wings
and jet propulsion. We see, too,
an aeroplane that has been 'born
of one of those rare flashes of

genius that renders all its contemporaries obsolescent at one
stroke'.

Boeing's first studies for a jet
bomber, begun in 1943, were
based upon conventional adapta-
tions of the B-29 Superfortress
to jet power. By 1945, as de
Havilland discovered with the
D.H. 106 Comet, the best aerodynamic arrangement of jet
engines in a large aeroplane
seemed to be to bury them in the
wings or fuselage. Then some
Boeing engineers, shortly after
VE day, went to Germany – and
out of their visit came the swept-
wing XB-47, having (like the
MiG-15 and Sabre) a 35 deg.
sweep-back.

The U.S.A.A.F. ordered two
prototypes in April 1946, and the
first of these was flown on 17
December 1947 – the 44th anniversary of the Wright brothers'
first powered flight. The 'flash of
genius' was not so much in individual design features of the B-
47, which in themselves were
each quite logical, but in the
boldness with which several of
them were united in a single airframe. The extremely thin wings,
to decrease drag, could house
neither fuel nor landing gear; the
spreading out of the engines in
pods along the wing, instead of
grouping them close to the fusel-

age; the development of a tandem landing gear, half in front and half behind the bomb bay; all combined in an airframe that appeared extremely radical when compared with the three conventional, straight-winged designs with which the B-47 was competing.

But the results were as remarkable as the aeroplane. It could not only out-pace the F-80 and F-84 fighters (one B-47 shot across the U.S.A. from coast to coast in February 1949 at over 600 m.p.h.; 966 km/hr.), but could out-*turn* them as well. Thus did the B-47 pioneer a configuration that has stood not only Boeing (with the 707 and

---

Specification of Boeing B-47E Stratojet

Engines: Six 6,000 lb. (2,722 kg.) s.t. General Electric J47-GE-25 turbojets.
Span: 116 ft. 0 in. (35·36 m.).
Length: 109 ft. 10 in. (33·48 m.).
Wing area: 1,428·0 sq. ft. (132·66 sq. m.).
Maximum take-off weight: 206,700 lb. (93,759 kg.).
Maximum speed: 606 m.p.h. (975 km/hr.) at 16,300 ft. (4,970 m.).
Service ceiling: 40,500 ft. (12,345 m.).
Range: 4,000 miles (6,437 km.).

---

747) but most other manufacturers of large jet aircraft in remarkably good stead to this day. Its other great achievement, which began in 1950, was to inaugurate the development of the famous Boeing 'flying boom' method of in-flight refuelling, with which it and later Strategic Air Command bombers can be kept in the air, at constant readiness, around the clock.

59. Vickers Viscount

How often is it remarked upon that the British government, as early as 1943, was apparently so confident of the outcome of World War 2 that it set up a body, the Brabazon Committee, to consider (and even issue specifications for) the kind of commercial transport aircraft that Britain would need when the war was over? Leaving aside the temptation to digress upon how many British governments, before or since, have had as much foresight as that, one cannot dispute that the exercise produced two absolute winners.

The first of these to fly was the 'Brabazon IIB' aircraft, designed by Rex Pierson of Vickers and bearing the company's Type number 630. Powered by two early Rolls-Royce Dart turbo-prop engines, it made its maiden flight at Wisley on 16 July 1948. It had originally been intended to use Armstrong Siddeley Mamba engines, but availability of the Dart enabled the seating capacity to be increased from twenty-four to thirty-two. The Viscount then nearly passed into limbo when British European Airways, at government insti-gation, cancelled its order in favour of the twin piston-engined Airspeed Ambassador.

But George Edwards (later Sir George Edwards, chairman of British Aircraft Corporation), who took over the Viscount's development from Pierson, re-mained convinced that the Dart would eventually offer the chance to 'stretch' the Viscount design; and he was quite right. A prototype of the fifty-three-passenger Series 700 Viscount was flown on 28 August 1950. Exactly a month earlier, the Type 630 had received its Certifi-cate of Airworthiness – the first for a turboprop airliner any-where in the world – and on 29 July B.E.A. borrowed it to help out with summer peak passen-gers, whose response to its smoothness, speed and comfort was unmistakable; and B.E.A.

lost no time in ordering twenty-six of the larger version.

Other orders soon followed from European airlines and, most significant of all, from T.C.A. in Canada and Capital Airlines in the United States. By 1956 there were more Viscounts flying in North America than in the whole of Europe – a most unaccustomed situation for a British aeroplane – and that same passenger appeal was apparent everywhere. The Viscount, including later versions seating up to seventy, went on to a pro-duction total that eventually reached 444, a figure that has been exceeded among turboprop civil aircraft only by the Fokker

---

**Specification of
Vickers Viscount 700D**

Engines: Four 1,740 e.h.p. Rolls-Royce Dart Mk. 510 turboprops.
Span: 93 ft. 8½ in. (28·56 m.).
Length: 81 ft. 10 in. (25·04 m.).
Wing area: 963·0 sq. ft. (89·47 sq. m.).
Maximum take-off weight: 64,500 lb. (29,257 kg.).
Maximum cruising speed: 334 m.p.h. (537 km/hr.) at 20,000 ft. (6,100 m.).
Service ceiling: 27,500 ft. (8,380 m.).
Range with maximum payload: 1,748 miles (2,813 km.).

F27 Friendship. Tribute is due as much to the Rolls-Royce Dart as to the Vickers airframe, and it is no coincidence that the Friendship, too, is powered by this outstanding engine.

60. Hawker Siddeley (de Havilland) Comet

The presence of the D.H.108 in the corner of the colour plate is a reminder that de Havilland's first submission for the Brabazon Committee's Type IV requirement, in 1945, was a tailless swept-wing design, for which the D.H.108 was intended to be a half-scale research aircraft. First flown on 15 May 1946, it was essentially the fuselage of a Vampire fighter, with Goblin jet engine, allied to swept-back wings, fin and rudder. Although it was soon realised that this layout would be uneconomical for a jet airliner, the D.H.108 continued to be a useful high-speed research aircraft, reaching a speed of 637 m.p.h. (1,025 km/hr.) before, on 27 September 1946, it ran into compressibility problems and broke up in the air, killing test pilot Geoffrey de Havilland.

In the modified third D.H. 108, however, his successor, John Cunningham, became on 6 September 1948, the first pilot to exceed the speed of sound in a British aircraft. Meanwhile, however, in September 1946 the de Havilland company had begun the design which was to emerge three years later as the D.H.106 Comet. With non-swept wings and tail, and four de Havilland Ghost turbojets buried in the wing roots, it was taken up by Cunningham on its first flight on 27 July 1949, and by the end of the year was making demonstration flights at cruising speeds of around 450 m.p.h. (724 km/hr.) – comparable to the maximum speeds of many World War 2 fighters.

When the thirty-six/forty-eight-seat Comet 1 entered service on B.O.A.C.'s London–Johannesburg route on 2 May 1952, it was the world's first jet airliner in commercial service. For almost two years the world was its oyster – until in April 1954 the latest in a series of unexplained and tragic crashes caused all Comets to be grounded. There followed a remarkable salvage effort by the Royal Navy, to recover enough fragments of one aircraft from the bed of the Mediterranean, and an incredible task of reassembly and testing by the Royal Aircraft Establishment, before metal fatigue was diagnosed as the cause of the trouble.

The much-improved Avon-powered Comet 4 appeared four years later, in time to snatch another 'first' from its new competitor, the Boeing 707: first jet airliner into service across the North Atlantic. What those four lost years cost the Comet's career, and the British aircraft industry, can never be calculated; but neither can the debt which aviation, in terms of technical knowledge and public safety, owes to the results of the investigation into the causes of one aeroplane's tragedy.

Specification of Hawker Siddeley Comet 4C

Engines: Four 10,500 lb. (4,763 kg.) s.t. Rolls-Royce Avon Mk.525B turbojets.
Span: 114 ft. 10 in. (35·00 m.).
Length: 118 ft. 0 in. (35·97 m.).
Wing area: 2,121·0 sq. ft. (197·05 sq. m.).
Maximum take-off weight: 162,000 lb. (73,500 kg.).
Typical cruising speed: 542 m.p.h. (872 km/hr.) at 31,000 ft. (9,450 m.).
Service ceiling: 39,000 ft. (11,890 m.).
Range with 19,630 lb. (8,900 kg.) payload: 2,590 miles (4,170 km.).

---

61. Lockheed Starfighter

The U.S. Air Force's 'Century Series' of fighters, beginning with the F-100 Super Sabre, marked the introduction, as normal, of combat aircraft capable of supersonic level flight. The fourth in this series, Lockheed's F-104 Starfighter, was the first operational warplane able to fly at twice the speed of sound for prolonged periods. It was also the first aircraft to hold, simultaneously, absolute world records for both speed and altitude (1,404·09 m.p.h.; 2,259·18 km/hr. and 91,244 ft.; 27,811 m., both set in 1958; the altitude figure was beaten in 1959 by another Starfighter).

First flown on 7 February 1954, the XF-104 departed completely from all theories about swept wings for high-speed flight, employing instead a thin, straight wing of very short span to produce a configuration that prompted Lockheed's publicists to describe it, with some justification, as 'a missile with a man in it'. Spectacular performer though it was, however, the early F-104 interceptor versions were a disappointment; but a hint of eventual potential appeared with the F-104C, produced as a fighter-bomber for Tactical Air

Command. Even so, U.S.A.F. procurement of the first four models totalled fewer than 300 aircraft.

What started the Starfighter's real success story was Germany's selection of the F-104G 'Super Starfighter', from fourteen contenders, in 1959. This multi-mission export version, re-designed, made stronger, fitted with manoeuvring flaps (which reduced its turning circle by one-third), better operational equipment and an uprated engine, eventually went into service with eight N.A.T.O. forces and

---

Specification of Lockheed CF-104 Starfighter

Engine: One 10,000/15,800 lb. (4,536/7,167 kg.) s.t. Orenda J79-OEL-7 afterburning turbojet.
Span: 21 ft. 11 in. (6·68 m.).
Length: 54 ft. 9 in. (16·69 m.).
Wing area: 196·1 sq. ft. (18·22 sq. m.).
Maximum take-off weight: 28,891 lb. (13,105 kg.).
Normal maximum speed: 1,320 m.p.h. (2,125 km/hr.) at 40,000 ft. (12,200 m.).
Combat ceiling: 55,000 ft. (16,765 m.).
Combat radius with two drop-tanks: 690 miles (1,110 km.).

---

became the subject of the largest international manufacturing programme since World War 2.

With derivatives, more than 2,000 were built, in Belgium, Canada, Germany, Holland, Italy and Japan, as well as those produced by Lockheed, and Italian production was still continuing (of the later F-104S) in 1976. Super Starfighters are in service as interceptors, fighter-bombers, reconnaissance and tactical nuclear strike aircraft, and only in the late 1970s or early 1980s will they be replaced by newer types such as the F-16 or the multi-role Tornado.

62. Boeing 707

With the 707, for the fourth time in its history the Boeing company developed a successful commercial transport out of an original military design, in this case following the airframe configuration first established with the B-47 Stratojet. It was not, as is so often said, the first United States jet transport to fly: that distinction belongs to the experimental Chase XC-123A, fitted with two twin-J47 pods from a B-47, which pre-dated the 707 prototype by more than three years. But it is the jet transport that transformed the pattern of global air transport in a remarkably short space of time.

It began life as a turbine-powered successor to the highly popular Boeing Stratocruiser, and made its first flight on 15 July 1954, the prototype being designated Model 367-80 (or, more familiarly, just 'Dash Eighty'). First customer was the U.S. Air Force, for tanker and transport versions, but it was offered to commercial operators in the summer of 1955. Nobody wanted to be first to buy it: jet airliners (notwithstanding the Comet) were new, they were expensive, their economics were unexplored – and, anyway, most major world airlines had only comparatively recently bought DC-7s or Super Constellations, the last word in piston-engined air transport.

But at last, in October 1955, Pan American took the plunge and ordered six – plus a similar quantity of Douglas's DC-8, which had still to fly. Then, equally suddenly, nobody wanted to be left out of the jet 'race', and within three years Boeing had orders for more than 180 Model 707s. Twenty years on, the 707-320 Intercontinental model is still in production, and total sales are in excess of 900.

The first 707s went into service with PanAm on the New York–London run on 26 October 1958, only a few weeks after the reintroduced Comet 4, and the same airline, a year later, began the first round-the-world service by jet. Almost overnight, the 707 and DC-8 brought about a revolution, their speed, comfort and reliability heralding a traffic boom unprecedented in aviation history. Meanwhile the remarkable 'Dash Eighty' continued to clock up the hours – and a 'modification record' second to none – in flight testing 'flying boom' refuelling gear, wing high-

---

**Specification of
Boeing 367-80**

Engines: Four 9,500 lb. (4,309 kg.) s.t. Pratt & Whitney JT3P turbojets.
Span: 129 ft. 8 in. (39·52 m.).
Length: 127 ft. 10 in. (38·96 m.).
Wing area: 2,400·0 sq. ft. (222·97 sq. m.).
Take-off weight: 190,000 lb. (86,182 kg.).
Maximum cruising speed: 550 m.p.h. (885 km/hr.).
Service ceiling: 43,000 ft. (13,100 m.).
Range: 3,530 miles (5,680 km.).

lift devices, landing gears, engines, radars, automatic landing equipment and many other features of benefit to the whole range of Boeing jet transport aircraft from the 707 onward – a performance from which it was at last honourably retired in the early 1970s.

63. Dassault Mirage

It is an odd coincidence that the two most successful military aeroplanes to be produced in Europe and the United States since World War 2 should both be named after intangibles: McDonnell Douglas's F-4 is an extremely substantial phantom, and there is many an Arab pilot to testify that there is very little that is illusory about Marcel Dassault's little delta-winged fighter.

Preceded by the tiny Mirage I, which flew in June 1955, the present family of Mirage fighters and bombers stems properly from the prototype Mirage III, which took to the air for the first time on 17 November 1956. Designed originally as an all-weather fighter for use from short, unprepared airstrips, the Mirage III is today also a tactical strike or reconnaissance aircraft,

and has been in continuous production since 1960. This production has also embraced sixty-two examples of the much-enlarged Mirage IV-A, with twin Atar engines and ability to carry a tactical nuclear weapon or conventional high-explosive bombs; and the more recent Mirage 5, a version with generally less sophisticated equipment but nevertheless a superb 'little war' combat aircraft able to carry a greater load of fuel or externally-mounted weapons.

Along the way there have also been such digressions as the vertical take-off Mirage III-V and Balzac prototypes, with centrally-mounted banks of lift-jet engines, but it is the basic Mirage III or 5 models that account for most of the 1,300 or so examples built or ordered up to 1976. These are truly world-wide in service: in Europe, they serve with the air forces of Belgium, France, Spain and Switzerland; in the Middle East with those of Abu Dhabi, Egypt, Israel, Lebanon, Libya and Saudia Arabia; in South America with those of the Argentine, Brazil, Colombia, Peru and Venezuela; and elsewhere with those of Australia, Pakistan, South Africa and Zaïre.

The Kfir, in production in

Israel in the mid-1970s, is a hybrid born of necessity. Denied, at different times, the import of Mirage 5s from France and Phantoms from America, Israel produced her own solution: put a Phantom engine into a Mirage airframe, make a few other airframe improvements, and fit home-grown electronics and missiles. Experts outside Israel had (up to early 1976) not had too close a look at the Kfir, but the result looks like a pretty effective warplane; though whether Dassault would agree with that viewpoint is another matter!

**Specification of
Dassault Mirage III-E**

Engine: One 9,436/14,110 lb. (4,280/6,400 kg.) s.t. SNECMA Atar 9C afterburning turbojet.
Span: 26 ft. 11½ in. (8·22 m.).
Length: 49 ft. 3½ in. (15·03 m.).
Wing area: 375·1 sq. ft. (34·85 sq. m.).
Maximum take-off weight: 29,760 lb. (13,500 kg.).
Maximum speed: 1,460 m.p.h. (2,350 km/hr.) at 39,375 ft. (12,000 m.).
Service ceiling: 55,775 ft. (17,000 m.).
Combat radius: 745 miles (1,200 km.).

---

64. McDonnell Douglas Phantom II

Arguably the best all-round combat aeroplane to have been produced anywhere in the world since 1945, the Phantom II perpetuates the name of an earlier McDonnell jet fighter produced for the U.S. Navy in 1946. This second Phantom, too, began life as an all-weather Navy fighter, but its versatility has since made it highly desirable also to the U.S. Air Force and Marine Corps, the Royal Air Force and Royal Navy, the Federal German Luftwaffe, and the air forces of Greece, Iran, Israel, Japan, South Korea, Spain and Turkey.

First ordered in 1954, it was still in production twenty-two years later, more than 4,500 then having been built. It made its first flight on 27 May 1958, and gave early indication of its performance by reaching a speed of 2·6 times the speed of sound while still under test. It has been the holder of numerous performance records, including past world records for speed and height, and can carry up to 16,000 lb. (7,250 kg.) of bombs, rockets, missiles or other ordnance – more than the normal wartime load of a four-engined Lancaster.

Versatility is reflected in its primary roles of interceptor, close-support, interdiction, electronic countermeasures and tactical strike and reconnaissance. The Phantom could scarcely be called pretty – it is brutishly large, and its unusual wing configuration led one American cynic to remark that McDonnell Douglas 'delivered them upside down' – but for a decade and a half there have been few warplanes that most front-line Western pilots would rather have under them.

**Specification of
McDonnell Douglas
F-4E Phantom II**

Engines: Two 11,870/17,900 lb. (5,385/8,119 kg.) s.t. General Electric J79-GE-17 afterburning turbojets.
Span: 38 ft. 5 in. (11·71 m.).
Length: 63 ft. 0 in. (19·20 m.).
Wing area: 530·0 sq. ft. (49·24 sq. m.).
Take-off weight: 57,400 lb. (26,036 kg.).
Maximum speed: 1,450 m.p.h. (2,334 km/hr.) at 36,000 ft. (11,000 m.).
Service ceiling: over 60,000 ft. (18,300 m.).
Maximum range: 1,860 miles (2,993 km.).

65. North American X-15

The fastest speeds and greatest heights at which man has ever flown, except in a space vehicle, have been achieved in the unique X-15, designed in 1955 to explore flight at speeds up to Mach 7 and heights up to 264,000 ft. (80,467 m.) and to gather prespaceflight data on re-entry, kinetic heating, stability and control problems. Three of them were built, and they were airlaunched from one of two specially-modified B-52 bombers, the first (unpowered) launch being made on 8 June 1959 and the second (powered) on 17 September the same year. Both flights were made by Scott Crossfield, test pilot of North American Aviation, a speed of 1,350 m.p.h. (2,173 km/hr.) being achieved on the second.

Milestones of 2,000 m.p.h. (3,219 km/hr.) were passed in August 1960, 3,000 m.p.h. (4,828 km/hr.) in April 1961, and on 9 November 1961 a speed of 4,093 m.p.h. (6,587 km/hr.) was reached. Other peaks of speed and height are given in more detail in Appendix 2, and reveal how closely the X-15 met or exceeded its original brief. Other, less apparent statistics might include the fact that the X-15 was virtually a flying fuel tank, carrying 18,000 lb. (8,165 kg.) of liquid oxygen and anhydrous ammonia propellant for the rocket motor; that most of its experimental flying was done *outside* the Earth's effective atmosphere; that the maximum temperature recorded on the aircraft's skin was 1,320 deg. F. (it had been designed to withstand 1,200 deg. F.); and that half of the twelve pilots assigned to the X-15 programme flew so high above the earth that they qualified for astronauts' 'wings'.

By August 1963 the X-15 had about reached the limit of its performance in its original form, and advantage was taken of an accident to the second aircraft to rebuild it in an improved form. It re-emerged as the X-15A-2, first flying in this new form on 28 June 1964. The most noticeable external differences were the new elliptical cockpit windows and expendable external fuel tanks, as shown in the colour illustration; later, the X-15A-2 received a Northrop-designed 'hot' nose (to act as a sensor for atmosphere exit and re-entry) and an overall coat of white ablative material to keep the skin temperature below 1,200 deg. F. By February 1966 the

three X-15s had made 156 flights, which totalled only just over twenty-four hours. Of this, 6 hours 29 minutes were at speeds above Mach 3; 4 hours 13 minutes above Mach 4; 56 minutes above Mach 5; and 11 seconds above Mach 6.

The number of flights had risen to 191 by February 1968, and in November of that year the X-15 research programme came to an end. One X-15, was, unfortunately, lost in a crash in November 1967, but the other two survive, one in the National Air and Space Museum in Washington and the other in the U.S.A.F. Museum at Wright-Patterson Air Force Base at Dayton, Ohio.

Specification of North American X-15A-2

Engine: One 57,000 lb. (25,855 kg.) s.t. Thiokol (Reaction Motors) XLR99-RM-2 single-chamber rocket motor.
Span: 22 ft. 0 in. (6·71 m.).
Length: 52 ft. 5 in. (15·98 m.).
Wing area: 200·0 sq. ft. (18·58 sq. m.).
Maximum launching weight: 50,914 lb. (23,095 kg.).
Performance: see main text and Appendix 2.

66. Hawker Siddeley P.1127 and Kestrel

Unique. That was the word for the Hawker P.1127 prototype when it was designed in 1957 and it was still the word for its operational offspring, the Hawker Siddeley Harrier, nineteen years later as this book was being written. Unique because its Rolls-Royce (originally Bristol Siddeley) Pegasus vectored-thrust engine is still the only one of its kind in the world, and unique because, until 1976, the Harrier was the world's only operational fixed-wing vertical take-off combat aircraft.

It is perhaps even more remarkable that the P.1127 should have had its genesis, as a private venture by Hawker, at the time when Defence Minister Duncan Sandys was cancelling almost everything in sight for the R.A.F. except missiles. Consequently it was designed to appeal to N.A.T.O. air forces as an eventual replacement for the Fiat G91, and it was two years before the British government, in June 1959, gave Hawkers a contract for two prototypes. In the event, N.A.T.O. shopped elsewhere, and it was the R.A.F. and the United States Marines that bought the Harrier.

The P.1127, of which six were eventually built, made its first vertical take-offs on 21 October 1960 (tethered) and 19 November 1960 (untethered), and the first transition between horizontal and hovering flight on 12 September 1961. Probably also unique was the formation of a special three-nation squadron, including ten test pilots from the R.A.F. (four), the U.S. Army and Luftwaffe (two each), and the U.S. Air Force and Navy (one each), to evaluate fully the pre-production version of the P.1127, known as the Kestrel. Nine of these were ordered for this purpose, the first of them flying on 7 March 1964, and

---

Specification of Hawker Siddeley Kestrel

Engine: One 15,200 lb. (6,895 kg.) s.t. Bristol Siddeley Pegasus 5 vectored-thrust turbofan.
Span: 22 ft. 11 in. (6·98 m.).
Length: 42 ft. 6 in. (12·95 m.).
Height: 10 ft. 9 in. (3·28 m.).
Maximum overload take-off weight: 17,000 lb. (7,711 kg.).
Maximum speed: approx. 725 m.p.h. (1,168 km/hr.) at sea level.
Maximum rate of climb at sea level: more than 20,000 ft. (6,100 m.)/min.

from April to November 1965 the Tripartite Squadron went fully into not only the performance of the Kestrel but the tactical implications of introducing this radically new class of warplane that needed no runways.

The outcome was the introduction into service on 1 April 1969 of the first squadron of R.A.F. Harriers – virtually a brand-new aeroplane compared with the P.1127 – and later by squadrons of the U.S. Marine Corps. In all respects, the P.-1127/Harrier was a worthy design to close the career of Sir Sydney Camm, one of Britain's greatest-ever aircraft designers.

67. Boeing 747

The most remarkable thing about the Boeing 747, perhaps, is that apart from its sheer size it is so *un*remarkable. It introduced no great aerodynamic breakthrough, no new advanced technology in airframe or engine manufacture; it was simply a bigger commercial transport aeroplane than anybody had ever built before.

The reason for this originated in the mid-1960s, when airline traffic was enjoying such a boom that it was apparent that within another ten years, there would either be needed a prodigious number of standard-sized jet transports – with the attendant airport handling and traffic control problems which that would entail – or a new conception of what constituted a 'standard' aircraft. Boldly, Boeing decided to redefine the standard.

A decade earlier, its Model 707 had been heralded as the 'first of the big jets'; now it embarked on a design more than four times the size and weight of the prototype 707, and a 200 million cu. ft. (5·66 million cu. m.) new building for its manufacture. Statistics of size for the new 747 are impressive, whether they be its sixteen-wheel main landing gear, to spread the strain of its great weight on existing runways, or its 187 ft. × 20 ft. × 8 ft. 4 in. (57·0 × 6·1 × 2·54 m.) passenger cabin dimensions. But perhaps one of the most telling is the realisation that at its (1976) maximum take-off weight the Boeing 747 weighs as much as 9½ war-time Lancaster bombers each carrying a 22,000 lb. 'Grand Slam' bomb.

First flown on 9 February 1969, the 747 entered service with Pan American Airways on 22 January 1970 – excellent testimony, incidentally, to a rapid and trouble-free certification programme. Early in its career, the 747 was quickly dubbed the 'Jumbo jet', a title that has now become a general one for other and later giant-size airliners such as the Lockheed TriStar and the McDonnell Douglas DC-10. The combined sales of all three types were well past the 750 mark by spring 1976, proof enough that the 'Jumbo' is here to stay.

Specification of Boeing 747-200

Engines: Four 48,570 lb. (22,030 kg.) s.t. Pratt & Whitney JT9D-7A turbofans.
Span: 195 ft. 8 in. (59·64 m.).
Length: 231 ft. 4 in. (70·51 m.).
Wing area: 5,500·0 sq. ft. (510·97 sq. m.).
Maximum take-off weight: 775,000 lb. (351,530 kg.).
Maximum speed: 608 m.p.h. (978 km/hr.) at 30,000 ft. (9,140 m.).
Cruise ceiling: 45,000 ft. (13,715 m.).
Typical range: 6,220 miles (10,000 km.).

---

68. Concorde

Concorde will go down in history for many reasons, and not least because it is the fruit of the first international agreement between the governments of two major aircraft-producing nations to join resources and evolve a new transport aeroplane for use by their respective national airlines. To do so took fourteen years and a prodigious amount of money, but it is to the eternal credit of the successive administrations of Britain and France, of varying shades of political opinion, that they did not succumb to political pressures – which were many – to abandon the whole project.

Concorde has had many ups and downs in its career, most of them of a political nature, and if anything has enabled it to survive them all it is surely the outstanding technological success of the aeroplane itself, proving all along the way that it could do just what its makers have always said it could do. Concorde was not the first supersonic transport in the world to fly – Russia's Tupolev Tu-144 beat it to this milestone by three months – but in a fourteen-year development period such a short time is neither here nor there. What is far more important is that, with nearly 4,000 flying hours 'on the clock' before receiving its certificate of airworthiness, Concorde is the most thoroughly-tested aeroplane ever to go into commercial service anywhere in the world.

In particular, its now-classic 'curved delta' wing was air-tested on another famous aircraft, the BAC 221, which in its original state was the Fairey Delta 2 which set the world's first air speed record in excess of 1,000 m.p.h. (1,609 km/hr.). Construction of the first two Concorde prototypes began in February 1965, and the first of these made its maiden flight on 2 March 1969. Simultaneously, production Concordes entered service on 21 January 1976 with British Airways (to Bahrain) and Air France (to Rio de Janeiro), followed in May 1976 by the opening of the all-important North Atlantic service to Washington.

At that date, Concorde still had two basic hurdles to overcome. One of these – its airport noise level – will almost certainly improve with time and continued research; the other – to attract orders from other airlines – may be more problematical. But one cannot help thinking back twenty years to the early Boeing 707s. Then, too, nobody wanted to be first . . .

Specification of Concorde

Engines: Four 38,050 lb. (17,260 kg.) s.t. Rolls-Royce/ SNECMA Olympus 593 Mk. 602 afterburning turbojets.
Span: 83 ft. 10 in. (25·56 m.).
Length: 203 ft. 9 in. (62·10 m.).
Wing area: 3,856·0 sq. ft. (358·25 sq. m.).
Maximum take-off weight: 400,000 lb. (181,435 kg.).
Maximum cruising speed: 1,354 m.p.h. (2,179 km/hr.) at 51,300 ft. (15,635 m.).
Service ceiling: approx. 60,000 ft. (18,300 m.).
Supersonic range with maximum payload: 3,869 miles (6,226 km.).

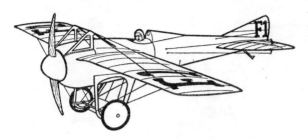

Fastest aeroplane to have flown before the outbreak of World War 1 was the
Deperdussin racer, which won the Gordon Bennett Trophy at Reims in 1913
and went on to set a world air speed record of 126·7 m.p.h. (203·85 km/hr.).

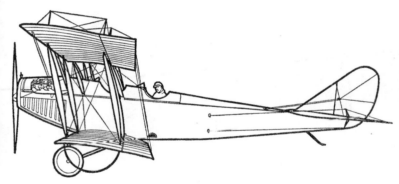

America's counterpart to the Avro 504 as a trainer, flying club and 'air circus'
aircraft was the Curtiss 'Jenny', so named from the letters JN of its makers'
designation, signifying a combination of the best features of the earlier Curtiss
Models J and N.

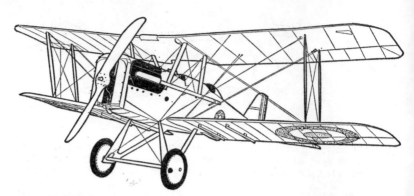

Probably the best design to emerge from Britain's Royal Aircraft Factory during World War 1, the S.E.5a single-seat fighter was a contemporary of the Sopwith Camel. It was liked particularly for its excellent performance at high altitude and its stability as a gun platform.

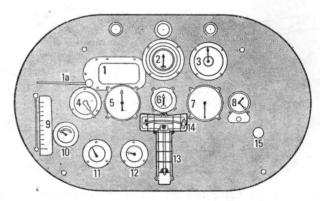

Cockpit instruments of Lindbergh's *Spirit of St Louis* Ryan monoplane. Key:

1.	Periscope and knob for	8.	Eight-day clock
1a.	extension and retraction	9.	Fuel mixer
2.	Earth inductor compass	10.	Oil pressure gauge
3.	Altimeter	11.	Fuel pressure gauge
4.	Magneto switch	12.	Oil temperature gauge
5.	Tachometer	13.	Fore and aft level gauge
6.	Turn and bank indicator	14.	Transverse level gauge
7.	Airspeed indicator	15.	Primer

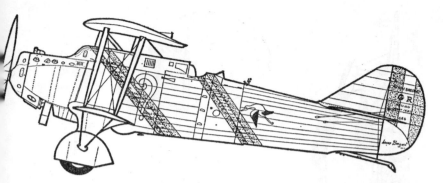

Two of France's greatest aviators between the wars were Dieudonné Costes and Joseph Le Brix. They were already famous as record-breakers when, between October 1927 and April 1928, they made a 35,000 mile (56,330 km) round-the-world flight from Paris in the Breguet XIX *Point d'Interrogation* (Question Mark).

Biplanes with negative (backward) stagger between their wings have several advantages over those with the more usual wing arrangement, yet have been comparatively rare in aviation history — one reason, perhaps, why those 'Staggerwing' Beech Model 17s which still survive from the 1930s and 1940s are today prized possessions of those U.S. pilots lucky enough to own one.

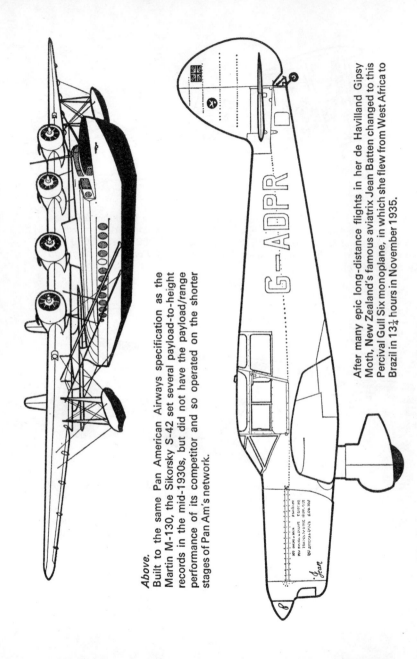

Above.
Built to the same Pan American Airways specification as the Martin M-130, the Sikorsky S-42 set several payload-to-height records in the mid-1930s, but did not have the payload/range performance of its competitor and so operated on the shorter stages of Pan Am's network.

After many epic long-distance flights in her de Havilland Gipsy Moth, New Zealand's famous aviatrix Jean Batten changed to this Percival Gull Six monoplane, in which she flew from West Africa to Brazil in 13¼ hours in November 1935.

G-ADPR

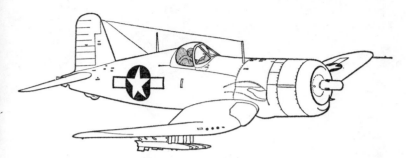

Unique among U.S. Navy World War 2 fighters with its inverted-gull wings, the Chance Vought Corsair was one of the finest aircraft of the Pacific war, achieving an 11 : 1 'kill ratio' over its Japanese opponents, who named it 'Whistling Death'. Its six-gun armament could be augmented, as shown here, with a battery of underwing rocket projectiles for attacking surface targets.

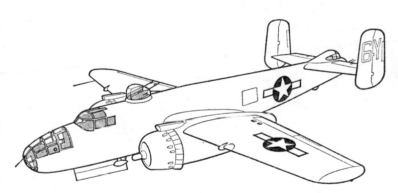

World War 2 produced many fine twin-engined bombers, on both sides, but North America's B-25 Mitchell will always be remembered for the audacious raid of 10 April 1942, in which a squadron of B-25Bs led by General 'Jimmy' Doolittle took off from the carrier *Hornet* to bomb the Japanese capital.

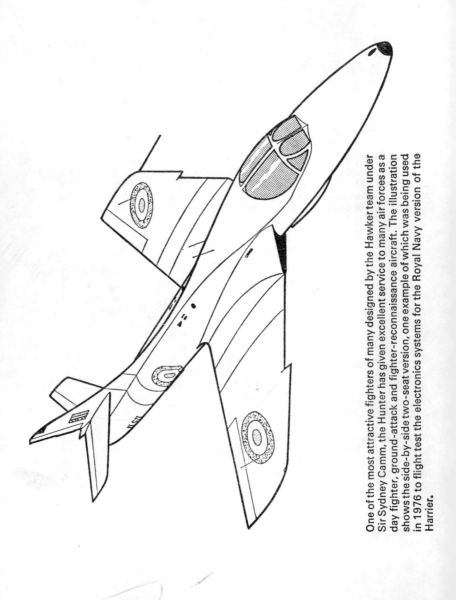

One of the most attractive fighters of many designed by the Hawker team under Sir Sydney Camm, the Hunter has given excellent service to many air forces as a day fighter, ground-attack and fighter-reconnaissance aircraft. The illustration shows the side-by-side two-seat version, one example of which was being used in 1976 to flight test the electronics systems for the Royal Navy version of the Harrier.

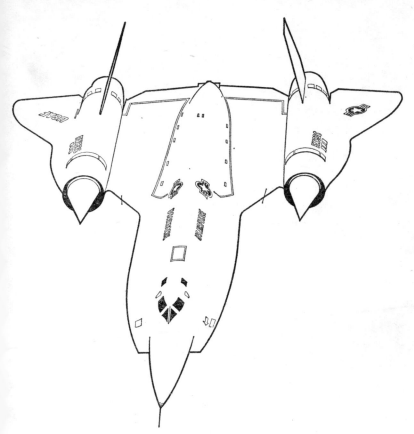

Holder of the world absolute air speed record (2,070·102 m.p.h.; 3,331·507 km/hr.) since May 1965, the Lockheed YF-12A experimental fighter became, in production form, the SR-71 strategic reconnaissance aircraft, capable of sustained flight at more than three times the speed of sound and altitudes of more than 80,000 ft. (24,400 m.). The YF-12A is illustrated; in July 1976 its eleven-year old record was beaten by an SR-71 which set up a new figure (subject to confirmation) of 2,200 m.p.h. (3,540 km/hr.), and a new world record for altitude in horizontal flight of 86,000 ft. (26,213 m.), also subject to confirmation.

APPENDIX I

LOG OF THE FLIGHT OF THE DOUGLAS WORLD CRUISERS,
APRIL TO SEPTEMBER 1924

Date	From/To	Dep.	Arr.	Flying Time (min.)	Distance (miles; km.)
April 1924					
6	Seattle–Prince Rupert	8.47	5.02	495	605; 974
10	Prince Rupert–Sitka	9.20	1.46	266	385; 619
13	Sitka–Seward	8.25	4.09	464	625; 1,006
15	Seward–Chignik	10.44	5.22	398	425; 684
19	Chignik–Dutch Harbor	11.01	6.25	446	390; 628
May 1924					
3	Dutch Harbor–Nazan	10.56	3.15	259	365; 588
9	Nazan–Attu	9.09	5.01	472	555; 893
*15/16	Attu–Nikolski	11.25	4.50	325	350; 563
17	Nikolski–Paramashiru	7.55	2.10	415	585; 941
19	Paramashiru–Hittokappu	7.30	2.50	440	595; 958
22	Hittokappu–Minato	5.25	10.30	305	485; 781
22	Minato–Kasumigaura	12.40	5.35	295	350; 563
June 1924					
1	Kasumigaura–Kushimoto	5.50	10.25	275	305; 491
2	Kushimoto–Kagoshima	12.50	7.01	371	360; 579
4	Kagoshima–Shanghai	7.05	4.15	550	550; 885
7	Shanghai–Tchinkoen Bay	7.50	12.20	270	350; 563
7	Tchinkoen Bay–Amoy	2.48	5.35	167	250; 402
8	Amoy–Hong Kong	10.11	1.35	204	310; 499
10	Hong Kong–Haiphong	11.15	6.41	446	495; 797
11	Haiphong–Tourane	11.55	5.50	365	410; 660
16	Tourane–Saigon	6.01	1.39	458	540; 869
18	Saigon–Kampongsana Bay	6.34	11.02	268	295; 475
18	Kampongsana Bay–Bangkok	12.10	4.12	242	290; 467
20	Bangkok–Tavoy	7.40	11.35	235	200; 322
20	Tavoy–Rangoon	2.42	5.50	188	295; 475

*International date line

Date	From/To	Dep.	Arr.	Flying Time (min.)	Distance (miles; km.)
June 1924					
25	Rangoon–Akyab	8.48	2.26	338	480; 772
26	Akyab–Chittagong	7.30	9.40	130	180; 290
26	Chittagong–Calcutta	12.05	3.22	197	265; 426
July 1924					
1	Calcutta–Allahabad	6.50	1.20	390	450; 724
2	Allahabad–Ambala	7.25	1.50	385	480; 772
3	Ambala–Multan	9.20	2.05	345	360; 579
4	Multan–Karachi	6.10	1.18	428	455; 732
7	Karachi–Chahbar	7.45	12.35	290	410; 660
7	Chahbar–Bander Abbas	2.35	6.40	245	365; 588
8	Bander Abbas–Bushire	5.40	9.45	245	390; 628
8	Bushire–Baghdad	11.25	5.55	390	530; 853
9	Baghdad–Aleppo	11.15	5.25	370	450; 724
10	Aleppo–Constantinople	6.02	1.40	458	560; 901
12	Constantinople–Bucharest	6.55	11.35	280	350; 563
13	Bucharest–Budapest	6.00	12.50	410	465; 748
13	Budapest–Vienna	2.20	4.20	120	113; 182
14	Vienna–Strasbourg	5.50	12.20	390	500; 805
14	Strasbourg–Paris	1.20	5.15	235	250; 402
16	Paris–London	11.00	2.07	187	215; 346
17	London–Brough	11.15	1.10	115	165; 266
30	Brough–Kirkwall	10.15	3.45	330	450; 724
Aug. 1924					
2	Kirkwall–Hornafjord	8.34	5.37	543	555; 893
5	Hornafjord–Reykjavik	9.12	2.15	303	290; 467
21	Reykjavik–Fredriksdahl	6.55	6.12	677	820; 1,320
24	Fredriksdahl–Ivigtut	10.55	1.07	132	165; 265
31	Ivigtut–Icy Tickle	8.25	3.20	415	560; 901
Sept. 1924					
2	Icy Tickle–Hawkes Bay	11.10	5.06	296	315; 507
3	Hawkes Bay–Pictou	11.10	5.44	394	430; 692
5	Pictou–Mere Point	11.15	5.20	365	460; 740
6	Mere Point–Boston	12.00	2.10	130	100; 161
8	Boston–New York	12.00	3.40	220	220; 354
9	New York–Aberdeen	9.35	1.15	220	160; 257
9	Aberdeen–Washington	2.30	3.55	85	70; 113
13	Washington–Dayton	10.50	5.35	405	400; 644
15	Dayton–Chicago	11.15	2.15	180	245; 394

Date	From/To	Dep.	Arr.	Flying Time (min.)	Distance (miles; km.)
Sept. 1924					
17	Chicago–Omaha	11.00	3.50	290	430; 692
18	Omaha–St Joseph	10.40	12.30	110	110; 177
18	St Joseph–Muskogee	1.25	5.20	235	270; 434
19	Muskogee–Dallas	12.30	4.15	225	245; 394
20	Dallas–Sweetwater	9.35	12.43	188	210; 338
20	Sweetwater–El Paso	1.50	7.10	380	390; 628
21	El Paso–Tucson	9.50	1.15	205	280; 451
22	Tucson–San Diego	7.20	11.25	245	390; 628
23	San Diego–Los Angeles	1.00	2.25	85	115; 185
25	Los Angeles–San Francisco	9.55	3.12	307	365; 588
27	San Francisco–Eugene	8.55	2.15	320	420; 676
28	Eugene–Vancouver	9.55	11.15	80	90; 145
28	Vancouver–Seattle	11.45	1.30	105	150; 241
	Totals			22,027	26,503; 42,652

(= 367 hrs 7 min.)

Average daily mileage: over 151 miles (243 km)
Average speed: 72·2 m.p.h. (116·2 km/hr.)

APPENDIX 2

PERFORMANCE ACHIEVEMENTS OF THE NORTH AMERICAN X-15

Speed: Date	Pilot	m.p.h.	km./hr.	Mach No.
12 May 1960	Joseph A. Walker (N.A.S.A.)	2,111	3,397	3·19
4 Aug. 1960	Joseph A. Walker (N.A.S.A.)	2,196	3,534	3·31
7 Feb. 1961	Major Robert M. White (U.S.A.F.)	2,275	3,661	3·50
7 Mar. 1961	Major Robert M. White (U.S.A.F.)	2,905	4,675	4·43
21 April 1961	Major Robert M. White (U.S.A.F.)	3,074	4,947	4·62
25 May 1961	Joseph A. Walker (N.A.S.A.)	3,300	5,311	4·90
23 June 1961	Major Robert M. White (U.S.A.F.)	3,603	5,798	5·27
12 Sept. 1961	Joseph A. Walker (N.A.S.A.)	3,614	5,816	5·25
28 Sept. 1961	Lt Cdr Forrest S. Petersen (U.S.N.)	3,620	5,826	5·25
11 Oct. 1961	Major Robert M. White (U.S.A.F.)	3,647	5,869	5·21
17 Oct. 1961	Joseph A. Walker (N.A.S.A.)	3,900	6,276	5·74
9 Nov. 1961	Major Robert M. White (U.S.A.F.)	4,093	6,587	6·04
*27 June 1962	Joseph A. Walker (N.A.S.A.)	4,104	6,605	5·92
*18 Nov. 1966	W. J. Knight	4,250	6,840	6·33
3 Oct. 1967	W. J. Knight	4,534	7,297	6·72

*By X-15A-2

Height: Date	Pilot	feet	miles	km.
12 Aug. 1960	Major Robert M. White (U.S.A.F.)	136,500	25·85	41·605
30 Mar. 1961	Joseph A. Walker (N.A.S.A.)	169,600	32·12	51·695
30 April 1962	Joseph A. Walker (N.A.S.A.)	246,700	46·72	75·195
17 July 1962	Major Robert M. White (U.S.A.F.)	314,750	59·61	95·935
19 July 1963	Joseph A. Walker (N.A.S.A.)	347,800	65·87	106·010
22 Aug. 1963	Joseph A. Walker (N.A.S.A.)	354,200	67·08	107·960

APPENDIX 3

Further details of many of the aircraft in this book, and of many other famous aircraft, may be found in the undermentioned volumes of the 'World Aircraft in Colour' series by the same author:

Pioneer Aircraft 1903–1914
Antoinette monoplanes
Avro 504
Blériot Type XI
Cody British Army Aeroplane No. 1
Curtiss June Bug, Gold Bug and Golden Flyer
Deperdussin monoplanes
Etrich Taube
Farman biplanes, including Farman III
Grahame–White Charabanc
Handley Page 'Yellow Peril'
Martinsyde monoplanes
Morane–Saulnier monoplanes
Roe triplane
Royal Aircraft Factory B.S.1 and S.E.4
Santos–Dumont 14bis and Demoiselle
Sikorsky Le Grand
Sopwith Tabloid
Voisin 1909 biplane
Wright Flyers I, II and III

Fighters 1914–1919
Albatros D types
Avro 504
Bristol Fighter and Scout
Curtiss 'Jenny'
de Havilland D.H.2

Etrich Taube
Farman 'Longhorn' and 'Shorthorn'
Fokker D types
Fokker Dr.I
Fokker E types
Morane Parasol
Nieuport 11 and 17
Royal Aircraft Factory B.E.2, F.E.2, S.E.5 and S.E.5a
Sopwith Camel, Dolphin, Pup, Salamander, Tabloid and Triplane
Spad VII and XIII
Vickers F.B.5 and F.B.9 'Gunbus'

Bombers 1914–1919
Blériot Type XI
Caproni Ca 1 to Ca 5
Curtiss Small America and Large America
de Havilland D.H.4, 9 and 9A
Gotha G types
Handley Page O/100, O/400 and V/1500
Royal Aircraft Factory R.E.8
Sikorsky Ilya Mourometz
Sopwith 1½-Strutter, Baby and Cuckoo
Vickers Vimy
Voisin bombers

Gloster Gladiator and Meteor
Grumman F4F Wildcat and F6F
    Hellcat
Hawker Hurricane, Tempest and
    Typhoon
Ilyushin Il-2
Junkers Ju 87 and Ju 88
Lockheed P-38 Lightning
Macchi C.200 and C.202
Messerschmitt Bf 109, Me 163 and
    Me 262
MiG-3
Mitsubishi 'Zero'
North American AT-6 Texan/
    Harvard and P-51 Mustang
Polikarpov I-16
Republic P-47 Thunderbolt
Supermarine Spitfire and Seafire
Yakovlev Yak-9

Bombers 1939–1945
Armstrong Whitworth Whitley
Avro Anson and Lancaster
Boeing B-17 Flying Fortress and
    B-29 Superfortress
Bristol Beaufighter and Blenheim
Consolidated B-24 Liberator
Curtiss SB2C Helldiver and C-46
    Commando
de Havilland Mosquito
Douglas C-47 Skytrain and SBD
    Dauntless
Dornier Do 17/215/217
Fairey Battle and Swordfish
Focke-Wulf Fw 200 Condor
Grumman TBF Avenger
Handley Page Halifax and
    Hampden
Heinkel He 111
Junkers Ju 52/3m, Ju 87 and Ju 88
North American B-25 Mitchell
Savoia–Marchetti S.M.79 Sparviero

Short Stirling and Sunderland
Supermarine Walrus
Vickers Wellington
Westland Lysander

Airliners since 1946
Aérospatiale Caravelle
Avro York
BAC VC10
Boeing 707, 727 and 747
Bristol Brabazon
Britten–Norman Islander
Concorde
Convair-liner
de Havilland Comet
Douglas DC-3, 4, 6 and 7
Fokker Friendship
Hawker Siddeley Trident
Ilyushin Il-14
Junkers Ju 52/3m
Lockheed Constellation, Super
    Constellation and TriStar
McDonnell Douglas DC-8, 9 and 10
Tupolev Tu-104, 114 and 144
Vickers Viking and Viscount

Fighters in Service
BAC Lightning
Dassault Mirage
Fiat G91
General Dynamics F-111
Grumman F-14 Tomcat
Hawker Hunter
Hawker Siddeley Gnat and
    Harrier
Lockheed F-104 Starfighter
McDonnell Douglas F-4 Phantom
    II and F-15 Eagle
MiG-17, 19, 21, 23 and 25
North American F-86 Sabre and
    F-100 Super Sabre

INDEX

Not in colour.